Implementing DevOps on AWS

Bring the best out of DevOps and build, deploy, and maintain applications on AWS

Veselin Kantsev

BIRMINGHAM - MUMBAI

Implementing DevOps on AWS

First published: January 2017

Production reference: 1190117

Published by Packt Publishing Ltd.
Livery Place
35 Livery Street
Birmingham
B3 2PB, UK.

ISBN 978-1-78646-014-1

www.packtpub.com

Credits

Author

Veselin Kantsev

Reviewer

Madhu Joshi

Commissioning Editor

Kartikey Pandey

Acquisition Editor

Namrata Patil

Content Development Editor

Abhishek Jadhav

Technical Editor

Mohd Riyan Khan

Copy Editor

Safis Editing

Project Coordinator

Judie Jose

Proofreader

Safis Editing

Indexer

Pratik Shirodkar

Graphics

Kirk D'Penha

Production Coordinator

Nilesh Mohite

About the Author

Veselin Kantsev is a DevOps professional and a Linux enthusiast who lives in London, UK.

His introduction to Linux was as a System Administrator back in 2006. His focus for the past few years has been mostly on cloud technologies and the transition of the community from an Ops to a DevOps culture.

He has worked with companies in various sectors such as Design, Media, and Finance, specializing in the migration of infrastructure onto AWS and the promotion of DevOps principles and practices.

About the Reviewer

Madhu Joshi, the VP of Cloud Services at Trillion Technology Solutions, has built high-profile websites in AWS for DoD, Verato, National Geospatial Agency (NGA), DHS FEMA, ProQuest Search Solutions, The Coca Cola Company, Food Network, Scripps, Special Olympics, Home and Garden TV, and Monumental Sports. He designed these sites to handle millions of visitors per month and has used industry best practices to provide peak capacity required to serve the global audience. He also has expertise in migrating large applications such as the KickApps social media platform and financial services from a traditional data center to Amazon's cloud.

I would like to thank Packt Publishing and Judie Jose for giving me the opportunity to review the book. This has turned out to be a great book, and I want to congratulate the author on putting on lot of hard work to make the book very useful. I am sure that the readers will have as much fun as I had reviewing it.

www.PacktPub.com

For support files and downloads related to your book, please visit www.PacktPub.com.

Did you know that Packt offers eBook versions of every book published, with PDF and ePub files available? You can upgrade to the eBook version at www.PacktPub.com and as a print book customer, you are entitled to a discount on the eBook copy. Get in touch with us at service@packtpub.com for more details.

At www.PacktPub.com, you can also read a collection of free technical articles, sign up for a range of free newsletters and receive exclusive discounts and offers on Packt books and eBooks.

https://www.packtpub.com/mapt

Get the most in-demand software skills with Mapt. Mapt gives you full access to all Packt books and video courses, as well as industry-leading tools to help you plan your personal development and advance your career.

Why subscribe?

- Fully searchable across every book published by Packt
- Copy and paste, print, and bookmark content
- On demand and accessible via a web browser

Customer Feedback

Thank you for purchasing this Packt book. We take our commitment to improving our content and products to meet your needs seriously—that's why your feedback is so valuable. Whatever your feelings about your purchase, please consider leaving a review on this book's Amazon page. Not only will this help us, more importantly it will also help others in the community to make an informed decision about the resources that they invest in to learn.

You can also review for us on a regular basis by joining our reviewers' club. **If you're interested in joining, or would like to learn more about the benefits we offer, please contact us**: customerreviews@packtpub.com.

Table of Contents

Preface

DevOps and **AWS** are two key subjects in the tech industry that have been steadily growing in popularity in recent years and for a good reason.

DevOps is gradually becoming the *de facto* methodology or framework and is adopted by organizations of all sizes. It has enabled technology teams to work more efficiently and made their work more rewarding by tightening the feedback loop between the developer and the end user. Team members enjoy a more pleasant, more productive work environment through much increased collaboration.

In this book, we will first examine the philosophy behind *DevOps*, then proceed with some practical examples of its most popular principles.

AWS is nowadays synonymous with *Cloud Computing*, sitting at the top of the industry charts with its 31% market share. Starting back in 2006, *Amazon Web Services* has evolved into a large, independent, sophisticated ecosystem in the *Cloud*. It is and has been launching new services at an astonishing rate. The *AWS* product categories range from raw compute and database resources to storage, analytics, *AI*, game development, and mobile services to *IoT* solutions.

We will use *AWS* as a platform to apply *DevOps* techniques on. In the chapters to follow, we will see how the convenience and elasticity of *AWS* greatly complements the innovative approach of *DevOps* to system administration and application development.

What this book covers

Chapter 1, *What Is DevOps and Should You Care?*, introduces the *DevOps* philosophy.

Chapter 2, *Start Treating Your Infrastructure as Code*, offers examples on how to deploy infrastructure as code using *Terraform* or *CloudFormation*.

Chapter 3, *Bring Your Infrastructure under Configuration Management*, demonstrates how to configure *EC2* instances using *SaltStack*.

Chapter 4, *Build, Test, and Release Faster with Continuous Integration*, describes the process of setting up a *CI* workflow using a *Jenkins CI* server.

Chapter 5, *Ever-Ready to Deploy Using Continuous Delivery*, shows how to extend a *CI* pipeline to produce deployment-ready *EC2 AMIs* using *Packer* and *Serverspec*.

Chapter 6, *Continuous Deployment - A Fully Automated Workflow,* Offers a fully automated workflow and completes the *CI/CDelivery* pipeline by adding the functionality needed for *AMI* deployment.

Chapter 7, *Metrics, Log Collection, and Monitoring,* introduces *Prometheus, Logstash, Elasticsearch,* and related *DevOps* tools.

Chapter 8, *Optimize for Scale and Cost,* offers advice on how to plan an *AWS* deployment with scalability and cost efficiency in mind.

Chapter 9, *Secure Your AWS Environment,* covers best practices in order to improve the security of an *AWS* deployment.

Chapter 10, *AWS Tips and Tricks,* contains a selection of useful tips for a beginner to an intermediate *AWS* users.

What you need for this book

The practical examples found in this book involve the use of *AWS* resources, thus an *AWS* account will be required.

The client-side tools used in the examples, such as the *AWS CLI* and *Terraform,* are supported on most common operating systems (*Linux/Windows/Mac OS*).

Who this book is for

This book is for system administrators and developers who manage AWS infrastructure and environments and are planning to implement DevOps in their organizations. Those aiming for the AWS Certified DevOps Engineer certification will also find this book useful. Prior experience of operating and managing AWS environments is expected.

Conventions

In this book, you will find a number of text styles that distinguish between different kinds of information. Here are some examples of these styles and an explanation of their meaning.

Code words in text, database table names, folder names, filenames, file extensions, pathnames, dummy URLs, user input, and Twitter handles are shown as follows: "We need to SSH into the node and retrieve the admin password stored in `/var/lib/jenkins/secrets/initialAdminPassword`."

A block of code is set as follows:

```
aws-region = "us-east-1"
vpc-cidr = "10.0.0.0/16"
vpc-name = "Terraform"
aws-availability-zones = "us-east-1b,us-east-1c"
```

When we wish to draw your attention to a particular part of a code block, the relevant lines or items are set in bold:

```
aws-region = "us-east-1"
vpc-cidr = "10.0.0.0/16"
vpc-name = "Terraform"
aws-availability-zones = "us-east-1b,us-east-1c"
```

Any command-line input or output is written as follows:

```
$ terraform validate
$ terraform plan
Refreshing Terraform state prior to plan...
...
Plan: 11 to add, 0 to change, 0 to destroy.
$ terraform apply
aws_iam_role.jenkins: Creating...
...
Apply complete! Resources: 11 added, 0 changed, 0 destroyed.
Outputs:
JENKINS EIP = x.x.x.x
VPC ID = vpc-xxxxx
```

New terms and **important words** are shown in bold. Words that you see on the screen, for example, in menus or dialog boxes, appear in the text like this: "We select **Pipeline** as a job type and pick a name for it."

Warnings or important notes appear in a box like this.

Tips and tricks appear like this.

Reader feedback

Feedback from our readers is always welcome. Let us know what you think about this book-what you liked or disliked. Reader feedback is important for us as it helps us develop titles that you will really get the most out of.

To send us general feedback, simply e-mail feedback@packtpub.com, and mention the book's title in the subject of your message.

If there is a topic that you have expertise in and you are interested in either writing or contributing to a book, see our author guide at www.packtpub.com/authors.

Customer support

Now that you are the proud owner of a Packt book, we have a number of things to help you to get the most from your purchase.

Downloading the example code

You can download the example code files for this book from your account at http://www.packtpub.com. If you purchased this book elsewhere, you can visit http://www.packtpub.com/support and register to have the files e-mailed directly to you.

You can download the code files by following these steps:

1. Log in or register to our website using your e-mail address and password.
2. Hover the mouse pointer on the **SUPPORT** tab at the top.
3. Click on **Code Downloads & Errata**.
4. Enter the name of the book in the **Search** box.
5. Select the book for which you're looking to download the code files.
6. Choose from the drop-down menu where you purchased this book from.
7. Click on **Code Download**.

Once the file is downloaded, please make sure that you unzip or extract the folder using the latest version of:

- WinRAR / 7-Zip for Windows
- Zipeg / iZip / UnRarX for Mac
- 7-Zip / PeaZip for Linux

The complete set of code can also be downloaded from the following GitHub repository: `https://github.com/PacktPublishing/Implementing-DevOps-on-AWS`.

Downloading the color images of this book

We also provide you with a PDF file that has color images of the screenshots/diagrams used in this book. The color images will help you better understand the changes in the output. You can download this file from `https://www.packtpub.com/sites/default/files/downloads/ImplementingDevOpsonAWS_ColorImages.pdf`.

Errata

Although we have taken every care to ensure the accuracy of our content, mistakes do happen. If you find a mistake in one of our books-maybe a mistake in the text or the code-we would be grateful if you could report this to us. By doing so, you can save other readers from frustration and help us improve subsequent versions of this book. If you find any errata, please report them by visiting `http://www.packtpub.com/submit-errata`, selecting your book, clicking on the **Errata Submission Form** link, and entering the details of your errata. Once your errata are verified, your submission will be accepted and the errata will be uploaded to our website or added to any list of existing errata under the Errata section of that title.

To view the previously submitted errata, go to `https://www.packtpub.com/books/content/support` and enter the name of the book in the search field. The required information will appear under the **Errata** section.

Piracy

Piracy of copyrighted material on the Internet is an ongoing problem across all media. At Packt, we take the protection of our copyright and licenses very seriously. If you come across any illegal copies of our works in any form on the Internet, please provide us with the location address or website name immediately so that we can pursue a remedy.

Please contact us at `copyright@packtpub.com` with a link to the suspected pirated material.

We appreciate your help in protecting our authors and our ability to bring you valuable content.

Questions

If you have a problem with any aspect of this book, you can contact us at `questions@packtpub.com`, and we will do our best to address the problem.

1

What is DevOps and Should You Care?

DevOps can be seen as an extension of the successful and well established **Agile** methodology. Bringing operations into the picture helps the advance from continuous (Agile) development to integration to deployment, but more importantly it helps build a better working environment, one with stronger cross-team relationships.

If I had to describe DevOps in one word, it would be collaboration. The genuine willingness of both the **Dev** and **Ops** camps to work together is the foundation, the most important aspect of the philosophy.

DevOps appears as the meeting point in the following diagram:

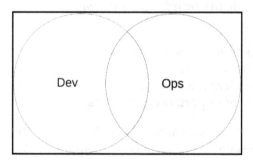

In this chapter we will go through the following topics:

- What is DevOps?
- Questions you should ask yourself before adopting it

What is DevOps?

So, let us examine the various principle characteristics of a DevOps environment.

What follows is a series of generally accepted definitions, invariably mixed with personal opinions – you have been warned.

A common goal

The alignment of effort toward increasing system performance and stability, reducing the time it takes to deploy or improving the overall quality of the product, will result in happier customers and proud engineers.

The goal needs to be repeated, clarified, and simplified until it is fully understood, argued against, and eventually committed to by everybody.

DevOps shifts focus away from self-interest and toward that goal. It directs praise at group achievements rather than those of the individual; *KPIs* and *Employee of the Month* initiatives perhaps not so much.

Allow people to look at the bigger picture past the realm of their cubicle. Trust them.

Shared knowledge (no silos)

The chances are you have already heard stories or read books about the notorious organizational silos.

In the worst case, it would be somebody who refuses to let go and often becomes the main bottleneck in a development life cycle. They can be fiercely territorial, safe-guarding what exclusive knowledge they might have in a given field, likely (I speculate) because this provides them with a sense of importance, further catering to their ego.

On the other hand, there are also examples of people who find themselves in a silo purely due to unfortunate circumstances. My respect goes out to the many engineers stuck with supporting inherited legacy systems all by themselves.

Fortunately, DevOps blurs such borders of expertise with concepts like **cross-functional teams** and **full-stack engineers**. It is important to note here that this does not translate into an opportunity to cut costs by expecting people to be tech ninja experts at every single thing (which in real life equates to preceding average). But, as in one of those Venn diagrams, it is the cross-over between a **Dev** and an **Ops** set of skills.

Silos are avoided by encouraging knowledge sharing. Peer reviews, demo stand-ups, or shared documentation are a few ways to ensure that no task or piece of know-how is limited to a specific person. You could even adopt **Pair Programming**. It seems a bit heavy, but it evidently works!

Trust and shared responsibility

Should developers be given production access?

There are good reasons for maintaining strict role-based permissions; one of them is security another is integrity. This standpoint remains valid for as long as we maintain the stereotype of the developer who is so used to working in **devlocal**; to them, concepts such as **passphrase-protected** SSH keys or not manually editing all of the files take a back seat.

In the era of DevOps, this is no longer the case. Shared knowledge and responsibility means operations engineers can rely on their developer colleagues to follow the same code of conduct when working in critical, production environments.

Dev and Ops teams have access to the same set of tools and environments. Deployments are no longer a special task reserved for the Ops team and scheduled days in advance.

In a team with such knowledge-sharing habits, I, as an operations engineer, can be confident about my Dev colleague's ability to perform my tasks, and vice versa.

Developers participate in the **on-call** rota, supporting the software they produce.

This is not to be seen as an additional burden, but as a sign of trust and an opportunity to increase collaboration. Nobody is *throwing code over the wall* anymore. Responsibility and a sense of autonomy motivates people to do more than is expected of them.

Respect

As we spend more time talking to each other about the challenges we face and the problems we are trying to solve, our mutual respect grows.

This manifests itself in developers seeking input from the Operations team from the early stages of the software development process or in Ops tools being built to meet developers' needs.

> *Ops who think like Devs. Devs who think like Ops*
> *— John Allspaw and Paul Hammond, Velocity*

A DevOps environment is built on such respect. It is a place where every opinion matters, where people can and do openly question decisions in the interest of the best solution to a problem. This is a powerful indicator of one's commitment toward the common goal I mentioned earlier.

Automation

To draw an overly simplified conclusion from A. Maslow's *Theory of Motivation*, you are less likely to think about poetry when hungry. In other words, a team with basic needs will be solving basic problems.

Automating routine and mundane tasks allows engineers to concentrate on the more complex, higher-value ones. Also, people get bored, cut corners, and make mistakes – computers tend not to do so.

Reproducible infrastructure

Describing infrastructure as code has the following advantages:

- It can be kept under version control
- It is easily shared with others to re-use or reproduce
- It serves as a very useful diary of what you did and how exactly you did it
- Provisioning cloud environments becomes trivial (for example, with Terraform or CloudFormation)
- It makes modern Configuration Management possible

At any rate, I suspect anybody managing more than 10 servers is already codifying infrastructure in some way or another.

Metrics and monitoring

> *Measure All The Things!*
> *– Actual DevOps slogan.*

Storage is cheap. Develop the habit of gathering copious amounts of measurements and making those easily accessible across your organization. The more visibility engineers have into the performance of their infrastructure and applications, the more adequate their decisions will be in critical situations.

Graphs can convey a great deal of information, look rather cool on big screens, and the human mind has been proven excellent at recognizing patterns.

Another important role of metrics data is in performance optimization.

> *The trickiest part of speeding up a program is not doing it, but deciding whether it's worth doing at all...Part of the problem is that optimization is hard to do well. It's frighteningly easy to devolve into superstitious ritual and rationalization.*
> *– Mature Optimization, Carlos Bueno*

To avoid falling prey to confirmation bias, you need an objective method of assessing your systems before and after attempting any optimization. Use those metrics; it is hard to argue with (valid) data.

On the subject of validity, please do calibrate your instruments regularly, sanity-check output and make sure what you think you are showing is what your colleagues think they are seeing (ref: `https://mars.jpl.nasa.gov/msp98/news/mco990930.html`).

Continuous Integration, Delivery, and Deployment

The **Observe, Orient, Decide,** and **Act (OODA)** loop is a concept developed by Col. J. Boyd that shows the value in one's ability to adapt to ever-changing circumstances.

Faced with unforgiving (and productive) competition, organizations should be able to rapidly react to dynamic market conditions.

This is probably best illustrated with the old Kodak and Netflix tales. The former after having been wildly successful is said to have failed to adapt to the new trends in their sector, causing the brand to gradually fade away. In contrast, Netflix keeps on skillfully molding their product to match the new ways in which we consume digital content. They completely transformed their infrastructure, shared some clever, new and somewhat controversial practices plus a ton of great software. Be like Netflix.

Continuous Integration and Delivery is essentially OODA in practice. Teams continuously integrate relatively small code changes, delivering releases more often, thus getting feedback from their users much quicker. The type of feedback needed by an organization to be able to adequately respond to an ever changing market.

None of the preceding suggests however that one should aim to become a *release hero,* rushing things into *Production,* setting it on fire twice a week. A *CI/CD* framework still implies the usual strict code review and test processes, despite how often you deploy. Though code reviews and testing require much less time and effort as typically the more frequent the deployments, the smaller the code changes.

Embracing failure

Naturally, more experimentation is likely to increase the probability of error.

I doubt this fact comes as a surprise to anybody; what might surprise you, however, is the advice to accept an additional, positive angle to failure.

Recall the video nerds from the previous section. Well, they didn't exactly breeze through all that change without casualties. I hereby spare you the Edison quotes; however, trial and error is indeed a valid form of the scientific method, and the DevOps processes serve as a great enabler to those who would agree.

In other words, an organization should encourage people to keep on challenging and improving the current state of affairs while also allowing them to openly talk about the times when things went wrong.

But dealing with experimentation failures is possibly the more romantic side of the story compared to the cold, harsh reality of day-to-day operations.

Systems fail. I would like to think most of us have come to accept that fact along with the chain of thought it provokes:

- we do not always know as much as we think we do:

  "Knowledge of the outcome makes it seem that events leading to the outcome should have appeared more salient to practitioners at the time than was actually the case...

  After an accident, practitioner actions may be regarded as errors or violations, but these evaluations are heavily   biased by hindsight and ignore the other driving forces..."
  – How Complex Systems Fail, R.I. Cook

Excelsior! Or how, in our long-standing pursuit of social dominance, we seem to have developed the convenient belief that following an event we not only know exactly what and how it happened but also why. This peculiar phenomenon has already been explained rather well by D. Kahneman in *Thinking Fast and Slow*; I will just add that indeed one often hears of overconfident characters who point fingers at their colleagues based on what appears to them as a coherent storyline.

The truth of the matter is this: we were not there. And keeping the details we now know and those known at the time separated is not an easy task.

- Blaming is of zero value:

Etsy and the likes in our community have shared enough observations to suggest that negative reinforcement as a strategy for reducing human error is less than optimal.

With the adoption of DevOps, we accept that people generally come to work every day with the intention to perform to the best of their abilities and in the interest of the organization. After an outage, we begin our analysis with the assumption that the operator has acted in the best possible way given the circumstances and information available to them at the time. We focus on what could have led to them making the given decisions, their thought process, the flow of events, and whether any of these can be improved.

- Resilience can be accumulated:

"What does not kill us..." **mithridatism** or Nassim Taleb's concept of **antifragility** are all expressive of the idea that we get better at dealing with negative experiences as we encounter them, and what's more, we should look for them every now and again.

We can train ourselves and our systems to recover from errors faster or even better to continue operating despite them. One way to achieve this is with controlled (and with practice, less controlled) outages.

With the right monitoring and auditing tools in place, every abnormal activity offers us a more intimate view of our applications and infrastructure.

Now that I have bestowed upon you, my dear reader, the secret to a better life through DevOps, let us concern ourselves with the latter part of the title of this chapter.

Should you care

I fail to see a reason why one should not. Some seven or so years have passed since the inception of the idea of DevOps, and the amount of evidence of its effectiveness has been growing steadily. Having the respected Agile framework at its base further adds to its credibility and perhaps helps explain a good part of its success.

That is not to say there are not considerations to be taken into account however. The critical thinker within you, would want to ask a question or two prior to embarking on such a cultural coup d'état.

Is this the right time?

Did you just finish adopting Lean or Agile Development? What else has been going on in the team? Is now the best time for yet another cry for change?

Altering our habits makes us uneasy; it takes some time to adjust. Your perseverance is laudable, and pursuing DevOps as the next level of team collaboration is often the right choice.

There is no need to give it up altogether; perhaps put it on hold for a moment.

Will it work?

Look around you. Those faces, those different personalities, can you picture them all together singing Kumbaya? Maybe yes, maybe no, or not yet.

Please do not e-mail an anonymous staff survey. Get everybody in a room, lay your DevOps propaganda out, and gauge their reactions.

You will need everyone to fully understand the concepts, acknowledge the challenges, and accept the sacrifices for this to work. There can neither be exceptions nor ambiguity.

All of this requires a great degree of cultural change, which a team should be prepared for.

Is it worth it?

What would it take to change the current mentality? How much of a disturbance you would need to cause? What degree of backlash do you expect?

While I am not suggesting this as an excuse to put up with the status quo, I beg you maintain a pragmatic view of the situation.

Your type of organization might be better suited for a process of evolution rather than a revolution.

Do you need it?

How would you score your current processes? Would you say your cross-team communication is satisfactory? You regularly meet business expectations? You have already automated most of your workflow?

It sounds like you are doing fine as it is; you might already have some DevOps in your team without realizing it. The point is that it could be a better use of resources if you were to concentrate on optimizing elsewhere, solving other, more pressing problems at this time.

Now that you have been through a yet another interpretation of the ideas behind DevOps, if you feel those match your way of thinking and the final few questions did not raise any concerns, then we can safely transition to the more technical topics where we put principles into practice.

Summary

First, we explored the main ideas contained in the DevOps philosophy, followed by a few questions aimed at helping you construct a more objective perspective when it comes to adopting DevOps within your organization.

We have seen that DevOps is an effective combination of some older, proven Agile concepts and other more recently developed ones, and that it teaches us how to build better teams who write better software, get results faster, and collaborate effortlessly in an environment that encourages experimentation without compromising stability.

Now that we have covered the theory, the next chapter takes us into the practical application of DevOps. We are going to begin with examples of deploying infrastructure as code in the cloud.

2
Start Treating Your Infrastructure as Code

Ladies and gentlemen, put your hands in the air, for Programmable Infrastructure is here!

Perhaps **Infrastructure-as-Code** (**IaC**) is not an entirely new concept considering how long Configuration Management has been around. Codifying server, storage, and networking infrastructure and their relationships, however, is a relatively recent tendency brought about by the rise of cloud computing. But let us leave Configuration Management for later and focus our attention on that second aspect of IaC.

You should recall from the previous chapter some of the benefits of storing all the things as code:

- Code can be kept under version control
- Code can be shared/collaborated on easily
- Code doubles as documentation
- Code is reproducible

That last point was a big win for me personally. Automated provisioning helped reduce the time it took to deploy a full-featured cloud environment from four hours down to one, and the occurrences of human error to almost zero (one shall not be trusted with an input field).

Being able to rapidly provision resources becomes a significant advantage when a team starts using multiple environments in parallel and needs those brought up or down on-demand. In this chapter, we examine in detail how to describe (in code) and deploy one such environment on AWS with minimal manual interaction.

To implement IaC in the cloud, we will look at two tools or services: **Terraform** and **CloudFormation**.

We will go through examples of the following:

- Configuring the tool
- Writing an IaC template
- Deploying a template
- Deploying subsequent changes to the template
- Deleting a template and removing the provisioned infrastructure

For the purpose of these examples, let us assume our application requires a **Virtual Private Cloud** (**VPC**) that hosts a **Relational Database Services** (**RDS**) backend and a couple of **Elastic Compute Cloud** (**EC2**) instances behind an **Elastic Load Balancer** (**ELB**). We will keep most components behind **Network Address Translation** (**NAT**), allowing only the load balancer to be accessed externally.

IaC using Terraform

One of the tools that can help deploy infrastructure on AWS is HashiCorp's Terraform (https://www.terraform.io). HashiCorp is that genius bunch that gave us Vagrant, Packer, and Consul. I would recommend you look up their website if you have not already.

Using **Terraform** (**TF**), we will be able to write a template describing an environment, perform a *dry run* to see what is about to happen and whether it is expected, deploy the template, and make any late adjustments where necessary-all of this without leaving the shell prompt.

Configuration

Firstly, you will need to have a copy of TF (https://www.terraform.io/downloads.html) on your machine and available on the CLI. You should be able to query the currently installed version, which in my case is 0.6.15:

```
$ terraform --version
  Terraform v0.6.15
```

Since TF makes use of the AWS APIs, it requires a set of authentication keys and some level of access to your AWS account. In order to deploy the examples in this chapter you could create a new **IdentityandAccess Management (IAM)** user with the following permissions:

```
"autoscaling:CreateAutoScalingGroup",
"autoscaling:CreateLaunchConfiguration",
"autoscaling:DeleteLaunchConfiguration",
"autoscaling:Describe*",
"autoscaling:UpdateAutoScalingGroup",
"ec2:AllocateAddress",
"ec2:AssociateAddress",
"ec2:AssociateRouteTable",
"ec2:AttachInternetGateway",
"ec2:AuthorizeSecurityGroupEgress",
"ec2:AuthorizeSecurityGroupIngress",
"ec2:CreateInternetGateway",
"ec2:CreateNatGateway",
"ec2:CreateRoute",
"ec2:CreateRouteTable",
"ec2:CreateSecurityGroup",
"ec2:CreateSubnet",
"ec2:CreateTags",
"ec2:CreateVpc",
"ec2:Describe*",
"ec2:ModifySubnetAttribute",
"ec2:RevokeSecurityGroupEgress",
"elasticloadbalancing:AddTags",
"elasticloadbalancing:ApplySecurityGroupsToLoadBalancer",
"elasticloadbalancing:AttachLoadBalancerToSubnets",
"elasticloadbalancing:CreateLoadBalancer",
"elasticloadbalancing:CreateLoadBalancerListeners",
"elasticloadbalancing:Describe*",
"elasticloadbalancing:ModifyLoadBalancerAttributes",
"rds:CreateDBInstance",
"rds:CreateDBSubnetGroup",
"rds:Describe*"
```

Please refer to this file for more information:
`https://github.com/PacktPublishing/Implementing-DevOps-on-AWS`
`/blob/master/5585_02_CodeFiles/Terraform/iam_user_policy.json`.

One way to make the credentials of the IAM user available to TF is by exporting the following environment variables:

```
$ export AWS_ACCESS_KEY_ID='user_access_key'
$ export AWS_SECRET_ACCESS_KEY='user_secret_access_key'
```

This should be sufficient to get us started.

Downloading the example code
Detailed steps to download the code bundle are mentioned in the Preface of this book.
The code bundle for the book is also hosted on GitHub at: `https://githu b.com/PacktPublishing/Implementing-DevOps-on-AWS`.
We also have other code bundles from our rich catalog of books and videos available at: `https://github.com/PacktPublishing/`. Check them out!

Template design

Before we get to coding, here are some of the rules:

- You could choose to write a TF template as a single large file or a combination of smaller ones
- Templates can be written in pure JSON or TF's own format
- TF will look for files with `.tf` or `.tf.json` extensions in a given folder and load them in alphabetical order
- TF templates are declarative, hence the order in which resources appear in them does not affect the flow of execution

A TF template generally consists of three sections: *resources*, *variables*, and *outputs*. As mentioned in the preceding section, it is a matter of personal preference how you arrange these; however, for better readability I suggest we make use of the TF format and write each section to a separate file. Also, while the file extensions are of importance, the filenames are up to you.

Resources

In a way, this file holds the main part of a template, as the resources represent the actual components that end up being provisioned. For example, we will be using the VPC Terraform resource, RDS, ELB and a few others to provision what roughly looks like this:

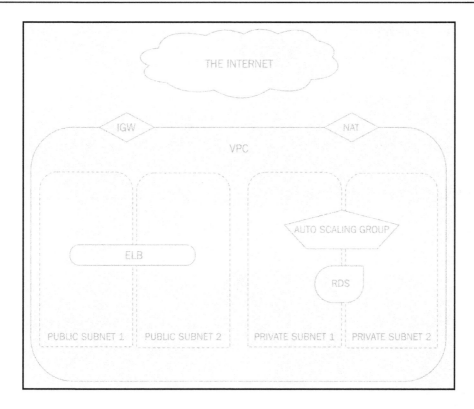

Since template elements can be written in any order, TF determines the flow of execution by examining any references that it finds (for example, a VPC should exist before an ELB that is said to belong to it is created). Alternatively, explicit flow control attributes such as depends_on are used, as we will observe shortly.

To find out more, let us go through the contents of the resources.tf file.

 Please refer to:
https://github.com/PacktPublishing/Implementing-DevOps-on-AWS
/blob/master/5585_02_CodeFiles/Terraform/resources.tf.

First, we tell Terraform what provider to use for our infrastructure:

```
# Set a Provider
  provider "aws"
{
  region = "${var.aws-region}"
}
```

You will notice that no credentials are specified, since we set them as environment variables earlier.

Now we can add the VPC and its networking components:

```
# Create a VPC
  resource "aws_vpc" "terraform-vpc"
{
  cidr_block = "${var.vpc-cidr}"

  tags
  {
    Name = "${var.vpc-name}"
  }
}

# Create an Internet Gateway
  resource "aws_internet_gateway" "terraform-igw"
{
  vpc_id = "${aws_vpc.terraform-vpc.id}"
}

# Create NAT
  resource "aws_eip" "nat-eip"
{
  vpc = true
}
```

So far, we have declared the VPC, its Internet and NAT gateways, plus a set of public and private subnets with matching routing tables.

It will help clarify the syntax if we examined some of those resource blocks, line by line:

```
resource "aws_subnet" "public-1" {
```

The first argument is the type of the resource followed by an arbitrary name:

```
vpc_id = "${aws_vpc.terraform-vpc.id}"
```

The `aws_subnet` resource named `public-1` has a `vpc_id` property, which refers to the `id` attribute of a different `aws_vpc` resource named `terraform-vpc`. Such references to other resources implicitly define the execution flow, that is to say, the VPC needs to exist before the subnet can be created:

```
cidr_block = "${cidrsubnet(var.vpc-cidr, 8, 1)}"
```

We will talk more about variables in a moment, but the format is `var.var_name as shown here`.

Here, we use the `cidrsubnet` function with the `vpc-cidr` variable, which returns a `cidr_block` to be assigned to the `public-1` subnet. Please refer to the TF documentation for this and other useful functions.

Next, we add a RDS to the VPC:

```
resource "aws_db_instance" "terraform" {
identifier = "${var.rds-identifier}"
allocated_storage = "${var.rds-storage-size}"
storage_type= "${var.rds-storage-type}"
engine = "${var.rds-engine}"
engine_version = "${var.rds-engine-version}"
instance_class = "${var.rds-instance-class}"
username = "${var.rds-username}"
password = "${var.rds-password}"
port = "${var.rds-port}"
vpc_security_group_ids = ["${aws_security_group.terraform-rds.id}"]
db_subnet_group_name = "${aws_db_subnet_group.rds.id}"
}
```

Here, we mostly see references to variables with a few calls to other resources.

Following the RDS is an ELB:

```
resource "aws_elb" "terraform-elb"
{
  name = "terraform-elb"
  security_groups = ["${aws_security_group.terraform-elb.id}"]
  subnets = ["${aws_subnet.public-1.id}",
"${aws_subnet.public-2.id}"]

listener
  {
    instance_port = 80
    instance_protocol = "http"
    lb_port = 80
    lb_protocol = "http"
```

```
    }

tags
  {
   Name = "terraform-elb"
  }
    }
```

Lastly, we define the EC2 Auto Scaling Group and related resources such as the Launch Configuration.

For the Launch Configuration we define the AMI and type of instance to be used, the name of the SSH keypair, EC2 security group(s) and the UserData to be used to bootstrap the instances:

```
resource "aws_launch_configuration" "terraform-lcfg" {
image_id = "${var.autoscaling-group-image-id}"
instance_type = "${var.autoscaling-group-instance-type}"
key_name = "${var.autoscaling-group-key-name}"
security_groups = ["${aws_security_group.terraform-ec2.id}"]
user_data = "#!/bin/bash \n set -euf -o pipefail \n exec 1> >(logger -s -t
$(basename $0)) 2>&1 \n yum -y install nginx; chkconfig nginx on; service
nginx start"

lifecycle {
create_before_destroy = true
}
```

The Auto Scaling Group takes the ID of the Launch Configuration, a list of VPC subnets, the min/max number of instances and the name of the ELB to attach provisioned instances to:

```
}
resource "aws_autoscaling_group" "terraform-asg" {
name = "terraform"
launch_configuration = "${aws_launch_configuration.terraform-lcfg.id}"
vpc_zone_identifier = ["${aws_subnet.private-1.id}",
"${aws_subnet.private-2.id}"]
min_size = "${var.autoscaling-group-minsize}"
max_size = "${var.autoscaling-group-maxsize}"
load_balancers = ["${aws_elb.terraform-elb.name}"]
depends_on = ["aws_db_instance.terraform"]
tag {
key = "Name"
value = "terraform"
propagate_at_launch = true
}
}
```

The preceding `user_data` shell script will install and start NGINX onto the EC2 node(s).

Variables

We have made great use of variables to define our resources, making the template as reusable as possible. Let us now look inside `variables.tf` to study these further.

Similarly to the resources list, we start with the VPC:

> Please refer to:
> https://github.com/PacktPublishing/Implementing-DevOps-on-AWS
> /blob/master/5585_02_CodeFiles/Terraform/variables.tf.

```
variable "aws-region" {
type = "string"
description = "AWS region"
}
variable "aws-availability-zones" {
type = "string"
description = "AWS zones"
}
variable "vpc-cidr" {
type = "string"
description = "VPC CIDR"
}
variable "vpc-name" {
type = "string"
description = "VPC name"
}
```

The syntax is as follows:

```
variable "variable_name" {
variable properties
}
```

`variable_name` is arbitrary, but needs to match relevant `var.var_name` references made in other parts of the template. For example, the `aws-region` variable will satisfy the `${var.aws-region}` reference we made earlier when describing the region of the `provider aws` resource.

We will mostly use `string` variables, but there is another useful type called **map** that can hold lookup tables. Maps are queried in a similar way to looking up values in a hash/dict (Please see: `https://www.terraform.io/docs/configuration/variables.html`).

Next comes RDS:

```
variable "rds-identifier" {
type = "string"
description = "RDS instance identifier"
}
variable "rds-storage-size" {
type = "string"
description = "Storage size in GB"
}
variable "rds-storage-type" {
type = "string"
description = "Storage type"
}
variable "rds-engine" {
type = "string"
description = "RDS type"
}
variable "rds-engine-version" {
type = "string"
description = "RDS version"
}
variable "rds-instance-class" {
type = "string"
description = "RDS instance class"
}
variable "rds-username" {
type = "string"
description = "RDS username"
}
variable "rds-password" {
type = "string"
description = "RDS password"
}
variable "rds-port" {
type = "string"
description = "RDS port number"
}
```

Lastly, we add our EC2 related variables:

```
variable "autoscaling-group-minsize" {
type = "string"
description = "Min size of the ASG"
}
variable "autoscaling-group-maxsize" {
type = "string"
description = "Max size of the ASG"
```

```
}
variable "autoscaling-group-image-id" {
type="string"
description = "EC2 AMI identifier"
}
variable "autoscaling-group-instance-type" {
type = "string"
description = "EC2 instance type"
}
variable "autoscaling-group-key-name" {
type = "string"
description = "EC2 ssh key name"
}
```

We now have the type and description of all our variables defined in `variables.tf`, but no values have been assigned to them yet.

TF is quite flexible with how this can be done. We could do it any of the following ways:

- Assign (default) values directly in `variables.tf`:
- variable "`aws-region`"{ `type = "string"description = "AWS region"default = 'us-east-1' }`
- Not assign a value to a variable, in which case TF will prompt for it at run time
- * Pass a `-var 'key=value'` argument directly to the TF command, like so:

`-var 'aws-region=us-east-1'`

- Store `key=value` pairs in a file
- Use environment variables prefixed with `TF_VAR`, as in `TF_VAR_ aws-region`

Using a `key=value` pairs file proves to be quite convenient within teams, as each engineer can have a private copy (excluded from revision control). If the file is named `terraform.tfvars` it will be read automatically by TF; alternatively, `-var-file` can be used on the command line to specify a different source.

Here is the content of our sample `terraform.tfvars` file:

Please refer to:
https://github.com/PacktPublishing/Implementing-DevOps-on-AWS
/blob/master/5585_02_CodeFiles/Terraform/terraform.tfvars.

```
autoscaling-group-image-id = "ami-08111162"
autoscaling-group-instance-type = "t2.nano"
```

```
autoscaling-group-key-name = "terraform"
autoscaling-group-maxsize = "1"
autoscaling-group-minsize = "1"
aws-availability-zones = "us-east-1b,us-east-1c"
aws-region = "us-east-1"
rds-engine = "postgres"
rds-engine-version = "9.5.2"
rds-identifier = "terraform-rds"
rds-instance-class = "db.t2.micro"
rds-port = "5432"
rds-storage-size = "5"
rds-storage-type = "gp2"
rds-username = "dbroot"
rds-password = "donotusethispassword"
vpc-cidr = "10.0.0.0/16"
vpc-name = "Terraform"
```

A point of interest is `aws-availability-zones`, as it holds multiple values that we interact with using the element and split functions, as seen in `resources.tf`.

Outputs

The third, mostly informational part of our template contains the TF Outputs. These allow selected values to be returned to the user when testing, deploying or after a template has been deployed. The concept is similar to how echo statements are commonly used in shell scripts to display useful information during execution.

Let us add outputs to our template by creating an `outputs.tf` file:

 Please refer to:
https://github.com/PacktPublishing/Implementing-DevOps-on-AWS
/blob/master/5585_02_CodeFiles/Terraform/outputs.tf.

```
output "VPC ID" {
value = "${aws_vpc.terraform-vpc.id}"
}

output "NAT EIP" {
value = "${aws_nat_gateway.terraform-nat.public_ip}"
}

output "ELB URI" {
value = "${aws_elb.terraform-elb.dns_name}"
}
output "RDS Endpoint" {
```

```
value = "${aws_db_instance.terraform.endpoint}"
}
```

To configure an output, you simply reference a given resource and its attribute. As shown in preceding code, we have chosen the ID of the VPC, the Elastic IP address of the NAT gateway, the DNS name of the ELB and the endpoint address of the RDS instance.

This section completes the template in this example. You should now have four files in your template folder: `resources.tf`, `variables.tf`, `terraform.tfvars`, and `outputs.tf`.

Operations

We shall examine five main TF operations:

- Validating a template
- Testing (dry-run)
- Initial deployment
- Updating a deployment
- Removal of a deployment

> In the following command line examples, Terraform is run within the folder that contains the template files.

Validation

Before going any further, a basic syntax check should be done with the `terraform validate` command. After renaming one of the variables in `resources.tf`, validate returns an `unknown variable` error:

```
$ terraform validate
Error validating: 1 error(s) occurred:
* provider config 'aws': unknown variable referenced: 'aws-region-1'.
define it with 'variable' blocks
```

Once the variable name has been corrected, re-running `validate` returns no output, meaning validation has passed.

Dry-run

The next step is to perform a test/dry-run execution with `terraform plan`, which displays what would happen during an actual deployment. The command returns a color-coded list of resources and their properties or more precisely, as follows:

```
$ terraform plan
Resources are shown in alphabetical order for quick scanning. Green
resources will be created (or destroyed and then created if an existing
resource exists), yellow resources are being changed in-place, and red
resources will be destroyed.
```

To literally get the picture of what the to-be-deployed infrastructure looks like, you could use `terraform graph`:

```
$ terraform graph > my_graph.dot
```

DOT files can be manipulated with the **Graphviz** open source software (Please see `http://www.graphviz.org`) or many online readers/converters. The following diagram is a portion of a larger graph representing the template we designed earlier:

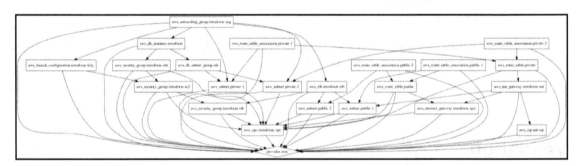

Terraform graph

Deployment

If you are happy with the plan and graph, the template can now be deployed using `terraform apply`:

```
$ terraform apply
aws_eip.nat-eip: Creating...
allocation_id: "" => "<computed>"
association_id: "" => "<computed>"
domain: "" => "<computed>"
instance: "" => "<computed>"
network_interface: "" => "<computed>"
```

```
private_ip: "" => "<computed>"
public_ip: "" => "<computed>"
vpc: "" => "1"
aws_vpc.terraform-vpc: Creating...
cidr_block: "" => "10.0.0.0/16"
default_network_acl_id: "" => "<computed>"
default_security_group_id: "" => "<computed>"
dhcp_options_id: "" => "<computed>"
enable_classiclink: "" => "<computed>"
enable_dns_hostnames: "" => "<computed>"
Apply complete! Resources: 22 added, 0 changed, 0 destroyed.
```

The state of your infrastructure has been saved to the following path. This state is required to modify and destroy your infrastructure, so keep it safe. To inspect the complete state, use the `terraform show` command.

```
State path: terraform.tfstate
Outputs:
ELB URI = terraform-elb-xxxxxx.us-east-1.elb.amazonaws.com
NAT EIP = x.x.x.x
RDS Endpoint = terraform-rds.xxxxxx.us-east-1.rds.amazonaws.com:5432
VPC ID = vpc-xxxxxx
```

At the end of a successful deployment, you will notice the `Outputs` we configured earlier and a message about another important part of *TF – the state file* (please refer to `https://www.terraform.io/docs/state/`):

TF stores the state of your managed infrastructure from the last time TF was run. By default, this state is stored in a local file named `terraform.tfstate`, but it can also be stored remotely, which works better in a team environment.

TF uses this local state to create plans and make changes to your infrastructure. Prior to any operation, TF does a refresh to update the state with the real infrastructure.

In a sense, the `state` file contains a snapshot of your infrastructure and is used to calculate any changes when a template has been modified. Normally, you would keep the `terraform.tfstate` file under version control alongside your templates. In a team environment however, if you encounter too many merge conflicts you can switch to storing the `state` file(s) in an alternative location such as S3 (please see: `https://www.terraform.io/docs/state/remote/index.html`).

Allow a few minutes for the EC2 node to fully initialize, then try loading the ELB URI from the preceding `Outputs` in your browser. You should be greeted by **nginx**, as shown in the following screenshot:

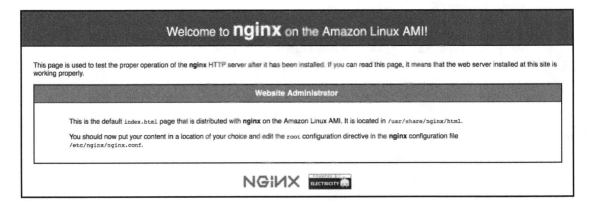

Updates

As per Murphy 's Law, as soon as we deploy a template, a change to it will become necessary. Fortunately, all that is needed for this is to update and re-deploy the given template.

Let's say we need to add a new rule to the ELB security group (shown in bold):

1. Update the `"aws_security_group"` `"terraform-elb"` resource block in `resources.tf`:

```
resource "aws_security_group" "terraform-elb" {
name = "terraform-elb"
description = "ELB security group"
vpc_id = "${aws_vpc.terraform-vpc.id}"
ingress {
from_port = "80"
to_port = "80"
protocol = "tcp"
cidr_blocks = ["0.0.0.0/0"]
}
ingress {
from_port = "443"
to_port = "443"
protocol = "tcp"
cidr_blocks = ["0.0.0.0/0"]
}
```

```
egress {
from_port = 0
to_port = 0
protocol = "-1"
cidr_blocks = ["0.0.0.0/0"]
}
}
```

2. Verify what is about to change:

```
$ terraform plan
...
~ aws_security_group.terraform-elb
ingress.#: "1" => "2"
ingress.2214680975.cidr_blocks.#: "1" => "1"
ingress.2214680975.cidr_blocks.0: "0.0.0.0/0" => "0.0.0.0/0"
ingress.2214680975.from_port: "80" => "80"
ingress.2214680975.protocol: "tcp" => "tcp"
ingress.2214680975.security_groups.#: "0" => "0"
ingress.2214680975.self: "0" => "0"
ingress.2214680975.to_port: "80" => "80"
ingress.2617001939.cidr_blocks.#: "0" => "1"
ingress.2617001939.cidr_blocks.0: "" => "0.0.0.0/0"
ingress.2617001939.from_port: "" => "443"
ingress.2617001939.protocol: "" => "tcp"
ingress.2617001939.security_groups.#: "0" => "0"
ingress.2617001939.self: "" => "0"
ingress.2617001939.to_port: "" => "443"
Plan: 0 to add, 1 to change, 0 to destroy.
```

3. Deploy the change:

```
$ terraform apply
...
aws_security_group.terraform-elb: Modifying...
ingress.#: "1" => "2"
ingress.2214680975.cidr_blocks.#: "1" => "1"
ingress.2214680975.cidr_blocks.0: "0.0.0.0/0" => "0.0.0.0/0"
ingress.2214680975.from_port: "80" => "80"
ingress.2214680975.protocol: "tcp" => "tcp"
ingress.2214680975.security_groups.#: "0" => "0"
ingress.2214680975.self: "0" => "0"
ingress.2214680975.to_port: "80" => "80"
ingress.2617001939.cidr_blocks.#: "0" => "1"
ingress.2617001939.cidr_blocks.0: "" => "0.0.0.0/0"
ingress.2617001939.from_port: "" => "443"
ingress.2617001939.protocol: "" => "tcp"
ingress.2617001939.security_groups.#: "0" => "0"
```

```
ingress.2617001939.self: "" => "0"
ingress.2617001939.to_port: "" => "443"
aws_security_group.terraform-elb: Modifications complete
...
Apply complete! Resources: 0 added, 1 changed, 0 destroyed.
```

> Some update operations can be destructive (please refer to
> http://docs.aws.amazon.com/AWSCloudFormation/latest/UserGuide/us
> ing-cfn-updating-stacks-update-behaviors.html). You should always
> check the CloudFormation documentation on the resource you are
> planning to modify to see whether a change is going to cause an
> interruption. TF provides some protection via the prevent_destroy life
> cycle property (please refer to
> https://www.terraform.io/docs/configuration/resources.html#preve
> nt_destroy).

Removal

This is a friendly reminder to always remove AWS resources after you are done experimenting with them to avoid any unexpected charges.

Before performing any delete operations, we will need to grant such privileges to the (terraform) IAM user we created in the beginning of this chapter. As a shortcut, you could temporarily attach the **AdministratorAccess** managed policy to the user via the AWS Console, as shown in the following figure:

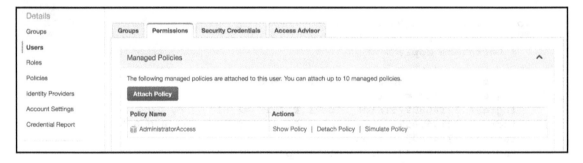

To remove the VPC and all associated resources that we created as part of this example, we will use `terraform destroy`:

```
$ terraform destroy
Do you really want to destroy?
Terraform will delete all your managed infrastructure.
There is no undo. Only 'yes' will be accepted to confirm.
Enter a value: yes
```

`Terraform` asks for a confirmation then proceeds to destroy resources, ending with the following:

```
Apply complete! Resources: 0 added, 0 changed, 22 destroyed.
```

Next, we remove the temporary admin access we granted to the IAM user by detaching the **AdministratorAccess** managed policy, as shown in the following screenshot:

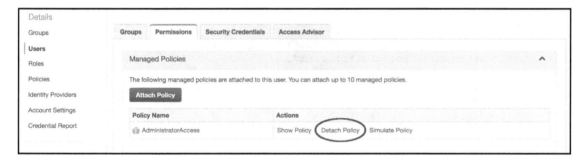

Then, verify that the VPC is no longer visible in the AWS Console.

IaC using CloudFormation

CloudFormation is an AWS service for deploying infrastructure as code. As before, we are going to describe our infrastructure via templates containing parameters (variables), resources, and outputs.

CloudFormation calls each deployed template a **Stack**. Creating, listing, updating, and deleting stacks is possible via the AWS Console, CLI, or API. In a small setup, you would probably deploy each of your stacks individually, but as your architecture becomes more complex, you can start nesting stacks. You would have a top-level or a parent stack (template) that invokes a number of sub-stacks. Nested stacks allow you to pass variables between them and, of course, save you the time of having to deploy each one individually.

Configuration

CloudFormation provides a GUI via the AWS Console; we however, are going to focus on the AWS CLI since it is most suitable for automating tasks in the future.

Depending on the OS you run, you could download an installer from `https://aws.amazon.com/cli/` or use Python PIP:

```
$ pip install awscli
$ aws --version
aws-cli/1.10.34 ...
```

We will need a set of API keys, so let's create a new IAM user called `cloudformation` with the following privileges:

```
"cloudformation:CancelUpdateStack",
"cloudformation:ContinueUpdateRollback",
"cloudformation:Create*",
"cloudformation:Describe*",
"cloudformation:EstimateTemplateCost",
"cloudformation:ExecuteChangeSet",
"cloudformation:Get*",
"cloudformation:List*",
"cloudformation:PreviewStackUpdate",
"cloudformation:SetStackPolicy",
"cloudformation:SignalResource",
"cloudformation:UpdateStack",
"cloudformation:ValidateTemplate",
"autoscaling:CreateAutoScalingGroup",
"autoscaling:CreateLaunchConfiguration",
"autoscaling:DeleteLaunchConfiguration",
"autoscaling:Describe*",
"autoscaling:UpdateAutoScalingGroup",
"ec2:AllocateAddress",
"ec2:AssociateAddress",
"ec2:AssociateRouteTable",
"ec2:AttachInternetGateway",
"ec2:AuthorizeSecurityGroupEgress",
"ec2:AuthorizeSecurityGroupIngress",
"ec2:CreateInternetGateway",
"ec2:CreateNatGateway",
"ec2:CreateRoute",
"ec2:CreateRouteTable",
"ec2:CreateSecurityGroup",
"ec2:CreateSubnet",
"ec2:CreateTags",
"ec2:CreateVpc",
```

```
"ec2:Describe*",
"ec2:Modify*",
"ec2:RevokeSecurityGroupEgress",
"elasticloadbalancing:CreateLoadBalancer",
"elasticloadbalancing:CreateLoadBalancerListeners",
"elasticloadbalancing:Describe*",
"elasticloadbalancing:ModifyLoadBalancerAttributes",
"elasticloadbalancing:SetLoadBalancerPoliciesOfListener",
"rds:CreateDBInstance",
"rds:CreateDBSubnetGroup",
"rds:Describe*"
```

Please refer to:
https://github.com/PacktPublishing/Implementing-DevOps-on-AWS
/blob/master/5585_02_CodeFiles/CloudFormation/iam_user_policy.
json.

You have the choice of using `aws configure`, which will prompt you for the API credentials, or if you prefer not to store them permanently, you could use an environment variable:

```
$ export AWS_ACCESS_KEY_ID='user_access_key'
$ export AWS_SECRET_ACCESS_KEY='user_secret_access_key'
```

CloudFormation templates do not store any AWS region information, so to avoid specifying it on the command line each time. It can be exported as well:

```
$ export AWS_DEFAULT_REGION='us-east-1'
```

With those environment variables in place, `awscli` should be ready for use.

Template design

CloudFormation templates are written in JSON and usually contain at least three sections (in any order): parameters, resources and outputs.

Unfortunately it is not possible to store these into separate files (with the exception of parameter values), so in this example we will work with a single template file named `main.json`.

Templates can be used locally or imported from a remote location (an S3 bucket is a common choice).

Parameters

Parameters add flexibility and portability to our Stack by letting us pass variables to it such as instance types, AMI ids, SSH keypair names and similar values which it is best not to hard-code.

Each parameter takes an arbitrary logical name (alphanumeric, unique within the template), description, type, and an optional default value. The available types are String, Number, CommaDelimitedList, and the more special AWS-specific type, such as AWS::EC2::KeyPair::KeyName, as seen in the preceding code.

The latter is useful for validation, as CloudFormation will check whether a key pair with the given name actually exists in your AWS account.

Parameters can also have properties such as AllowedValues, Min/MaxLength, Min/MaxValue, NoEcho and other (please see http://docs.aws.amazon.com/AWSCloudFormation/latest/UserGuide/parameters-section-structure.html).

There is a limit of 60 parameters per template.

Let us examine the parameters found at the top of our template:

Please refer to:
https://github.com/PacktPublishing/Implementing-DevOps-on-AWS/blob/master/5585_02_CodeFiles/CloudFormation/main.json.

```
"Parameters" : {
"vpcCidr" : {
"Description" : "VPC CIDR",
"Type" : "String"
},
"vpcName" : {
"Description" : "VPC name",
"Type" : "String"
},
"awsAvailabilityZones" : {
"Description" : "List of AZs",
"Type" : "CommaDelimitedList"
},
"publicCidr" : {
"Description" : "List of public subnet CIDRs",
"Type" : "CommaDelimitedList"
},...
"rdsInstanceClass" : {
```

```
"Description" : "RDS instance class",
"Type" : "String",
"AllowedValues" : ["db.t2.micro", "db.t2.small", "db.t2.medium"]
},
"rdsUsername" : {
"Description" : "RDS username",
"Type" : "String"
},
"rdsPassword" : {
"Description" : "RDS password",
"Type" : "String",
"NoEcho" : "true"
},
...
"autoscalingGroupKeyname" : {
"Description" : "EC2 ssh key name",
"Type" : "AWS::EC2::KeyPair::KeyName"
},
"autoscalingGroupImageId" : {
"Description" : "EC2 AMI ID",
"Type" : "AWS::EC2::Image::Id"
}
}
```

We have used the following:

- `CommaDelimitedList`, which we will conveniently query later with a special function
- `AllowedValues` and `MinValue` to enforce constraints
- `NoEcho` for passwords or other sensitive data
- Some AWS-specific types to have CloudFormation further validate input

You will notice that there are no values assigned to any of the preceding parameters.

To maintain a reusable template, we will store values in a separate file (`parameters.json`):

Please refer to:
https://github.com/PacktPublishing/Implementing-DevOps-on-AWS
/blob/master/5585_02_CodeFiles/CloudFormation/parameters.json.

```
[
{
"ParameterKey": "vpcCidr",
"ParameterValue": "10.0.0.0/16"
},
```

```
{
"ParameterKey": "vpcName",
"ParameterValue": "CloudFormation"
},
{
"ParameterKey": "awsAvailabilityZones",
"ParameterValue": "us-east-1b,us-east-1c"
},
{
"ParameterKey": "publicCidr",
"ParameterValue": "10.0.1.0/24,10.0.3.0/24"
},
{
"ParameterKey": "privateCidr",
"ParameterValue": "10.0.2.0/24,10.0.4.0/24"
},
{
"ParameterKey": "rdsIdentifier",
"ParameterValue": "cloudformation"
},
{
"ParameterKey": "rdsStorageSize",
"ParameterValue": "5"
},
{
"ParameterKey": "rdsStorageType",
"ParameterValue": "gp2"
},
{
"ParameterKey": "rdsEngine",
"ParameterValue": "postgres"
},...
```

Resources

You are already familiar with the concept of resources and how they are used to describe different pieces of infrastructure.

Regardless of how resources appear in a template, CloudFormation will follow its internal logic to decide the order in which these get provisioned.

The syntax for declaring a resource is as follows:

```
"Logical ID" : {
"Type" : "",
"Properties" : {}
}
```

IDs need to be alphanumeric and unique within the template.

The list of CloudFormation resource types and their properties can be found here:
`http://docs.aws.amazon.com/AWSCloudFormation/latest/UserGuide/aws-template-reso`
`urce-type-ref.html`

The max number of resources a template can have is 200. Reaching that limit, you will need to split a template into smaller ones and possibly look into nested stacks.

Back to our example, as per tradition we start by creating a VPC and its supporting elements such as subnets, Internet gateway and NAT gateway:

Please refer to:
`https://github.com/PacktPublishing/Implementing-DevOps-on-AWS`
`/blob/master/5585_02_CodeFiles/CloudFormation/main.json`.

```json
"Resources" : {
"vpc" : {
"Type" : "AWS::EC2::VPC",
"Properties" : {
"CidrBlock" : { "Ref" : "vpcCidr" },
"EnableDnsSupport" : "true",
"EnableDnsHostnames" : "true",
"Tags" : [ { "Key" : "Name", "Value" : { "Ref" : "vpcName" } } ]
}
},
"publicSubnet1" : {
"Type" : "AWS::EC2::Subnet",
"Properties" : {
"AvailabilityZone" : { "Fn::Select" : [ "0", {"Ref" :
"awsAvailabilityZones"} ] },
"CidrBlock" : { "Fn::Select" : [ "0", {"Ref" : "publicCidr"} ] },
"MapPublicIpOnLaunch" : "true",
"Tags" : [ { "Key" : "Name", "Value" : "Public" } ],
"VpcId" : { "Ref" : "vpc" }
}
},
...
"internetGateway" : {
"Type" : "AWS::EC2::InternetGateway",
"Properties" : {
"Tags" : [ { "Key" : "Name", "Value" : { "Fn::Join" : [ " - ", [ { "Ref" :
"vpcName" }, "IGW" ] ] } } ]
}
},
"internetGatewayAttachment" : {
```

```
"Type" : "AWS::EC2::VPCGatewayAttachment",
"Properties" : {
"InternetGatewayId" : { "Ref" : "internetGateway" },
"VpcId" : { "Ref" : "vpc" }
}
},
"natEip" : {
"Type" : "AWS::EC2::EIP",
"Properties" : {
"Domain" : "vpc"
}
},
"natGateway" : {
"Type" : "AWS::EC2::NatGateway",
"Properties" : {
"AllocationId" : { "Fn::GetAtt" : ["natEip", "AllocationId"]},
"SubnetId" : { "Ref" : "publicSubnet1" }
},
"DependsOn" : "internetGatewayAttachment"
},
```

Note some of the `CloudFormation` functions used in the preceding code:

- `"Fn::Select"` in `"CidrBlock" : { "Fn::Select" : [ "0", {"Ref" : "publicCidr"} ] }`, which allows us to query the `CommaDelimitedList` type parameters we set earlier
- `"Fn::Join"`, for concatenating strings
- `"Fn::GetAtt"`, for retrieving resource attributes

Also, the `DependsOn` property of the `natGateway` resource allows us to set explicit conditions on the order of execution. In this case, we are saying that the Internet Gateway resource needs to be ready (attached to the VPC) before the NAT Gateway is provisioned.

After the VPC, let's add RDS:

```
"rdsInstance" : {
"Type" : "AWS::RDS::DBInstance",
"Properties" : {
"DBInstanceIdentifier" : { "Ref" : "rdsIdentifier" },
"DBInstanceClass" : { "Ref" : "rdsInstanceClass" },
"DBSubnetGroupName" : { "Ref" : "rdsSubnetGroup" },
"Engine" : { "Ref" : "rdsEngine" },
"EngineVersion" : { "Ref" : "rdsEngineVersion" },
"MasterUserPassword" : { "Ref" : "rdsPassword" },
"MasterUsername" : { "Ref" : "rdsUsername" },
"StorageType" : { "Ref" : "rdsStorageType" },
```

```
"AllocatedStorage" : { "Ref" : "rdsStorageSize" },
"VPCSecurityGroups" : [ { "Ref" : "rdsSecurityGroup" } ],
"Tags" : [ { "Key" : "Name", "Value" : { "Ref" : "rdsIdentifier" } } ]
}}
```

Then add the ELB:

```
...
"elbInstance" : {
"Type" : "AWS::ElasticLoadBalancing::LoadBalancer",
"Properties" : {
"LoadBalancerName" : "cloudformation-elb",
"Listeners" : [ { "InstancePort" : "80", "InstanceProtocol" : "HTTP",
"LoadBalancerPort" : "80", "Protocol" : "HTTP" } ],
    "SecurityGroups" : [ { "Ref" : "elbSecurityGroup" } ],
    "Subnets" : [ { "Ref" : "publicSubnet1" }, { "Ref" : "publicSubnet2" }
],
    "Tags" : [ { "Key" : "Name", "Value" : "cloudformation-elb" } ]
    }
    }
```

And add the EC2 resources:

```
...
"launchConfiguration" : {
"Type" : "AWS::AutoScaling::LaunchConfiguration",
"Properties" : {
"ImageId" : { "Ref": "autoscalingGroupImageId" },
"InstanceType" : { "Ref" : "autoscalingGroupInstanceType" },
"KeyName" : { "Ref" : "autoscalingGroupKeyname" },
"SecurityGroups" : [ { "Ref" : "ec2SecurityGroup" } ]
```

We still use a `UserData` shell script to install the NGINX package; however, the presentation is slightly different this time. `CloudFormation` is going to concatenate the lines using a new line character as a delimiter then encode the result in `Base64`:

```
"UserData" : {
"Fn::Base64" : {
"Fn::Join" : [
"\n",
[
"#!/bin/bash",
"set -euf -o pipefail",
"exec 1> >(logger -s -t $(basename $0)) 2>&1",
"yum -y install nginx; chkconfig nginx on; service nginx start"
]
]
}
```

```
        }
      }
    }
```

We use `DependsOn` to ensure the RDS instance goes in before `autoScalingGroup`:

```
"autoScalingGroup" : {
"Type" : "AWS::AutoScaling::AutoScalingGroup",
"Properties" : {
"LaunchConfigurationName" : { "Ref" : "launchConfiguration" },
"DesiredCapacity" : "1",
"MinSize" : "1",
"MaxSize" : "1",
"LoadBalancerNames" : [ { "Ref" : "elbInstance" } ],
"VPCZoneIdentifier" : [ { "Ref" : "privateSubnet1" }, { "Ref" :
"privateSubnet2" } ],
"Tags" : [ { "Key" : "Name", "Value" : "cloudformation-asg",
"PropagateAtLaunch" : "true" } ]
},
"DependsOn" : "rdsInstance"
}
```

Outputs

Again, we will use these to highlight some resource attributes following a successful deployment. Another important feature of `Outputs`, however, is that they can be used as input parameters for other templates (stacks). This becomes very useful with nested stacks.

Once declared, `Outputs` cannot be subsequently updated on their own. You will need to modify at least one resource in order to trigger an Output update.

We add the `VPC ID`, `NAT IP` address and `ELB DNS` name as `Outputs`:

Please refer to:
https://github.com/PacktPublishing/Implementing-DevOps-on-AWS
/blob/master/5585_02_CodeFiles/CloudFormation/main.json.

```
"Outputs" : {
"vpcId" : {
"Description" : "VPC ID",
"Value" : { "Ref" : "vpc" }
},
"natEip" : {
```

```
"Description" : "NAT IP address",
"Value" : { "Ref" : "natEip" }
},
"elbDns" : {
"Description" : "ELB DNS",
"Value" : { "Fn::GetAtt" : [ "elbInstance", "DNSName" ] }
}
}
```

Currently, a template can have no more than 60 Outputs.

Operations

If you have been following along, you should now have a `main.json` and a `parameters.json` in your current folder. It is time to put them to use, so here are a few operations we are going to perform:

- Validate a template
- Deploy a stack
- Update a stack
- Delete a stack

Template validation

First things first, a basic check of our JSON template with `validate-template`:

```
$ aws cloudformation validate-template --template-body file://main.json
{
"Description": "Provisions EC2, ELB, ASG and RDS resources",
"Parameters": [
{
"NoEcho": false,
"Description": "EC2 AMI ID",
"ParameterKey": "autoscalingGroupImageId"
}
```

If there's no errors, the CLI returns the parsed template. Note that we could have just as easily pointed to a remote location using `--template-url` instead of `-template-body`.

Deploying a Stack

To deploy our template (stack), we will use `create-stack`. It takes an arbitrary name, the location of the template, and the file containing parameter values:

```
$ aws cloudformation create-stack --stack-name cfn-test --template-body
  file://main.json --parameters file://parameters.json
{
"StackId": "arn:aws:cloudformation:us-east-1:xxxxxx:stack/cfn-
test/xxxxxx"
}
```

CloudFormation starts creating the stack and no further output is returned. To get progress information on the CLI, use `describe-stacks`:

```
$ aws cloudformation describe-stacks --stack-name cfn-test
{
"Stacks": [
{
"StackId": "arn:aws:cloudformation:us-east-xxxxxx:stack/cfn-test/xxxxxx"
...
"CreationTime": "2016-05-29T20:07:17.813Z",
"StackName": "cfn-test",
"NotificationARNs": [],
"StackStatus": "CREATE_IN_PROGRESS",
"DisableRollback": false
}
]
}
```

And for even more details, use `describe-stack-events`.

After a few minutes (based on our small template) `StackStatus` changes from `CREATE_IN_PROGRESS` to `CREATE_COMPLETE` and we are provided the requested `Outputs`:

```
$ aws cloudformation describe-stacks --stack-name cfn-test
"Outputs": [
{
"Description": "VPC ID",
"OutputKey": "vpcId",
"OutputValue": "vpc-xxxxxx"
},
{
"Description": "NAT IP address",
"OutputKey": "natEip",
"OutputValue": "x.x.x.x"
},
{
```

```
"Description": "ELB DNS",
"OutputKey": "elbDns",
"OutputValue": "cloudformation-elb-xxxxxx.us-east-1.elb.amazonaws.com"
}
],
"CreationTime": "2016-05-29T20:07:17.813Z",
"StackName": "cfn-test",
"NotificationARNs": [],
"StackStatus": "CREATE_COMPLETE",
"DisableRollback": false
```

At this point, the `elbDNS` URL should return the nginx welcome page, as shown here:

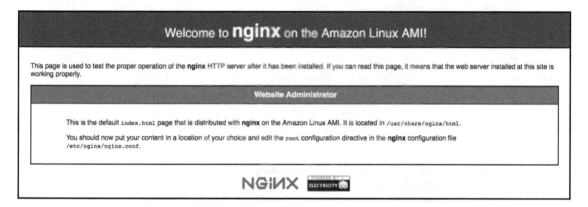

If not, you might need to allow some more time for the EC2 node to fully initialize.

Updating a stack

`CloudFormation` offers two ways of updating a deployed stack.

Some update operations can be destructive (please refer to
`http://docs.aws.amazon.com/AWSCloudFormation/latest/UserGuide/us`
`ing-cfn-updating-stacks-update-behaviors.html`). You should always
check the `CloudFormation` documentation on the resource you are
planning to modify to see whether a change is going to cause any
interruption.

If you would like to quickly deploy a minor change, then all you need to do is modify the template file and deploy it directly with `update-stack`:

```
$ aws cloudformation update-stack --stack-name cfn-test
  --template-body file://main.json
  --parameters file://parameters.json
```

Otherwise, a good practice would be to use `Change Sets` to preview stack changes before deploying them. For example, let us update the rules in the ELB security group as we did before:

1. Modify the `main.json` template (add another rule to `elbSecurityGroup`):

```
"elbSecurityGroup" : {
"Type" : "AWS::EC2::SecurityGroup",
"Properties" : {
"SecurityGroupIngress" : [ { "ToPort" : "80", "FromPort" : "80",
"IpProtocol" : "tcp", "CidrIp" : "0.0.0.0/0" },
  { "ToPort" : "443", "FromPort" : "443", "IpProtocol" :
    "tcp", "CidrIp" : "0.0.0.0/0" } ]
```

2. Create a Change Set:

```
$ aws cloudformation create-change-set
  --change-set-name updatingElbSecGroup
  --stack-name cfn-test --template-body file://main.json
  --parameters file://parameters.json
```

3. Preview the Change Set:

```
$ aws cloudformation describe-change-set
  --change-set-name updatingSecGroup
  --stack-name cfn-test
```

4. Execute the Change Set:

```
$ aws cloudformation execute-change-set --change-set-name
  updatingSecGroup --stack-name cfn-test
```

Whether via a Change Set or updating directly, if you are simply modifying parameter values (`parameters.json`) you can skip re-uploading the template (`main.json`) with `--use-previous-template`.

Deleting a stack

In order to tidy up after our experiments, we will need to grant temporary Admin privileges to the CloudFormation IAM user (the same procedure as in the earlier TF section); run `delete-stack`:

```
$ aws cloudformation delete-stack --stack-name cfn-test
```

Then revoke the Admin privileges.

Summary

In this chapter, we looked at the importance and usefulness of Infrastructure as Code and ways to implement it using `Terraform` or AWS `CloudFormation`.

We examined the structure and individual components of both a TF and a CF template then practiced deploying those onto AWS using the CLI. I trust that the examples we went through have demonstrated the benefits and immediate gains from the practice of deploying infrastructure as code.

So far, however, we have only done half the job. With the provisioning stage completed, you will naturally want to start configuring your infrastructure, and that is what we are going to do in the next chapter on *Configuration Management*.

3
Bringing Your Infrastructure Under Configuration Management

As hinted at the end of the previous chapter, there is some more work to be done before we can claim to have fully implemented IaC.

The first step was to describe the hardware side of our infrastructure in code; now it is time to look at the software or configuration aspect of it.

Let us say we have provisioned a few EC2 nodes and would like to have certain packages installed on them, and relevant configuration files updated. Prior to **Configuration Management (CM)** tools gaining popularity, such tasks would have been performed manually by an engineer either following a checklist, running a collection of shell scripts, or both. As you can imagine, such methods do not scale well as they generally imply one engineer setting up one server at a time.

In addition, checklists or scripts:

- Are hard to write when it comes to configuring a host plus a full application stack running on it
- Are usually targeted at a given host or application and are not very portable
- Get progressively harder to comprehend the further you get from the person who originally wrote them
- Build scripts tend to get executed only once, usually at the time a host is provisioned, thus configuration starts to drift from that moment on

Fortunately, not many people use these nowadays, as Configuration Management has become a common practice. Let us examine some of the benefits:

- CM allows us to declare the desired state of a machine once and then reproduce that state as often as necessary
- Powerful abstraction takes care of specifics such as environment, hardware, and OS type, allowing us to write reusable CM code
- The declared machine state code is easy to read, comprehend, and collaborate on.
- A CM deployment can be performed on tens, hundreds, or thousands of machines simultaneously

In this age of DevOps, there are a variety of CM tools to choose from. You might have already heard of Puppet, Chef, Ansible, OpsWorks, or the one we are going to use- **SaltStack (the Salt Open project)**.

All of these are well developed, sophisticated CM solutions with active communities behind them. I find it hard to justify any reported claims of one being better than the rest as they all do the job pretty well, each with its own set of strengths and weaknesses. So which one you use, as is often the case, is up to personal preference.

Regardless of the tool you end up using, I would like to stress the importance of two points: naming conventions and code reusability.

Following naming conventions when writing code is an obvious win as it guarantees other people will be able to understand your work with less effort. In addition to writing code however, CM involves executing it against your nodes and this is where naming also becomes important. Imagine you had four servers: **leonardo**, **donatello**, **michelangelo**, and **raphael**. Two of those are your frontend layer and two the backend, so you sit down and write your Configuration Management manifests respectively: *webserver-node* and *database-node*. So far, so good, given the number of hosts you can launch your CM tool and easily tell it to run the relevant manifest against each of them.

Now imagine 50, then 100 hosts, within a similar flat-naming schema, and you start to see the problem. As the size and complexity of your infrastructure grows, you will need a host-naming convention that naturally forms a hierarchy. Hostnames such as *webserver-{0..10}*, *db-{0..5}* and *cache-{0..5}* can be further grouped into frontend and backend and then represented in a structured, hierarchical way. Such a way of grouping nodes based on role or other properties is extremely useful when applying Configuration Management.

Code reusability should already be on your mind when you start writing CM code (manifests). You will find that there are generally two ways of approaching this task. You could write a large, say, web server piece which contains instructions on how to set up the firewall, some CLI tools, NGINX, and PHP on a node, or you could break it down into smaller parts like iptables, utils, NGINX, PHP, and so on.

In my opinion, the latter design adds some overhead when writing the manifests, but the benefit of reusability is substantial. Instead of writing large sets of declarations dedicated to each server type, you maintain a collection of generic, small ones and cherry-pick from them to suit the machine in question.

To illustrate:

```
manifests: everything_a_websrv_needs, everything_for_a_db, cache_main
nodes: web01, db01, cache01
CM_execution: web01=(everything_a_websrv_needs),
db01=(everything_for_a_db), cache01=(cache_main)
```

Or better:

```
manifests: iptables, utils, nginx, postgresql, redis, php
nodes: web01, db01, cache01
CM_execution: web01=(iptables,utils,nginx,php),
db01=(iptables,utils,postgresql), cache01=(iptables,utils,redis)
```

Introduction to SaltStack

SaltStack (see `https://saltstack.com/`), first released in 2011, is an automation suite which offers Configuration Management plus standard and/or event-driven orchestration. It is commonly used in a master-minion setup, where a master node provides centralized control across a compute estate. It is known for its speed and scalability thanks to the fast and lightweight message bus (**ZeroMQ**) used for communication between the salt-master and minions. It can also be used in an agentless fashion, where the minions are controlled over SSH, similarly to how Ansible operates.

SaltStack is written in Python and is easily extensible. You can write your own modules for it, attach long-running processes to its event bus, and inject raw Python code in unusual places.

The master-minion model is quite powerful, offers a lot of flexibility, and is the recommended approach if you are looking after anything more than a few dev nodes and want to take advantage of all the features SaltStack has to offer.

 More on how to get a salt-master up and running can be found here: `https://docs.saltstack.com/en/latest/topics/configuration/index.html`

In our case, we are going to explore the power of Configuration Management using SaltStack in a standalone or masterless mode. We will reuse parts of the Terraform template from the previous chapter to launch a set of EC2 resources, bootstrap a SaltStack minion and have it configure itself to serve a web application.

Provided all goes well, we should end up with a fully configured web server (EC2 node) behind a load-balancer (EC2 ELB).

Here is our task-list:

1. Prepare our SaltStack development environment.
2. Write the configuration that we would like SaltStack to apply to our node(s).
3. Compose the Terraform template describing our infrastructure.
4. Deploy the infrastructure via Terraform and let SaltStack configure it.

Preparation

SaltStack Configuration Management is performed using the following main components:

- **States** are the files which describe the desired state of a machine. Here we write instructions for installing packages, modifying files, updating permissions, and so on.
- **Pillars** are the files in which we define variables to help make States more portable and flexible.
- **Grains** are pieces of information gathered on the minion host itself. These include details about the OS, environment, the hardware platform, and others.
- The **Salt File Server** stores any files, scripts, or other artifacts which may be referenced in the States.
- The Salt Top file(s) are used to map States and/or Pillars to minions.

In a master-minion setup, all of these components except the Grains would be hosted on and made available to the minions by the salt-master (other backends are also supported).

We are planning to run Salt in masterless mode however, meaning that we will need a way to transfer any States, Pillars, and related files from our local environment to the minion. Git? Good idea. We will write all Salt code locally, push it to a Git repository, and then have it checked out onto each minion at boot time.

As for choosing a Git hosting solution, Github or Bitbucket are excellent services, but giving our minion EC2 nodes access to these will involve some key handling. In comparison, **CodeCommit** (the AWS Git solution) offers a much smoother integration with EC2 instances via IAM Roles.

Let us start by creating a new IAM user and a CodeCommit Git repository. We will be using the user's access keys to create the repository and a SSH key to clone and work with it:

1. In the AWS Console, create an IAM user (write down the generated access keys) and attach the **AWSCodeCommitFullAccess** built-in / **Managed** IAM policy to it as shown in the following screenshot:

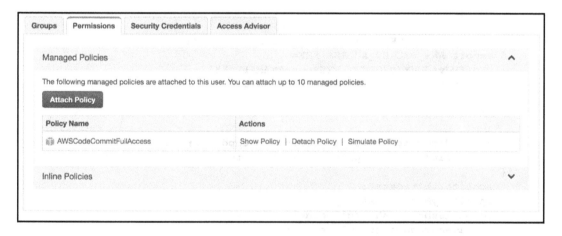

2. On the same page, switch to the **Security Credentials** tab and click on the **Upload SSH public key** as shown in the following screenshot:

3. Configure `awscli`:

```
$ export AWS_ACCESS_KEY_ID='AKIAHNPFB9EXAMPLEKEY'
$ export AWS_SECRET_ACCESS_KEY=
  'rLdrfHJvfJUHY/B7GRFTY/VYSRwezaEXAMPLEKEY'
$ export AWS_DEFAULT_REGION='us-east-1'
```

4. Create a repository:

```
$ aws codecommit create-repository --repository-name salt
  --repository-description "SaltStack repo"
{
"repositoryMetadata": {
"repositoryName": "salt",
"cloneUrlSsh": "ssh://git-codecommit.us-
 east-1.amazonaws.com/v1/repos/salt",
"lastModifiedDate": 1465728037.589,
"repositoryDescription": "SaltStack repo",
"cloneUrlHttp":
"https://git-codecommit.us-east-1.amazonaws.com/v1/repos/salt",
"creationDate": 1465728037.589,
"repositoryId": "d0628373-d9a8-44ab-942a-xxxxxx",
"Arn": "arn:aws:codecommit:us-east-1:xxxxxx:salt",
"accountId": "xxxxxx"
}
}
```

5. Clone the new repository locally:

```
$ git clone ssh://SSH_KEY_ID@git-codecommit.us-
east-1.amazonaws.com/v1/repos/salt
Cloning into 'salt'...
warning: You appear to have cloned an empty repository.
Checking connectivity... done.
```

Here, `SSH_KEY_ID` is the one we saw after uploading a public key in step 2.

> For more options on connecting to CodeCommit see
> `http://docs.aws.amazon.com/codecommit/latest/userguide/setting-u`
> `p.html`

We are ready to start populating our empty, new Salt repository.

Writing Configuration Management code

For SaltStack to help us configure our node as a web server, we need to tell it what one of those should look like. In Configuration Management terms, we need to describe the desired state of the machine.

In our example, we will be using a combination of SaltStack States, Pillars, Grains, and Top files to describe the processes of:

- Creating Linux user accounts
- Installing services (NGINX and PHP-FPM)
- Configuring and running the installed services

States

A State contains a set of instructions which we would like to be applied to our EC2 minion(s). We will use `/srv/salt/states` on the minion as the root of the Salt State tree. States can be stored in there in the form of a single file, for example `/srv/salt/states/mystate.sls`, or organized into folders like so `/srv/salt/states/mystate/init.sls`. Later on, when we request that `mystate` is executed, Salt will look for either a `state_name.sls` or a `state_name/init.sls` in the root of the *State Tree*. I find the second approach tidier as it allows for other state-related files to be kept in the relevant folder.

We begin the Configuration Management of our web server node with a state for managing Linux user accounts. Inside our Salt Git repository, we create `states/users/init.sls`:

 Please refer to:
`https://github.com/PacktPublishing/Implementing-DevOps-on-AWS`
`/tree/master/5585_03_CodeFiles/CodeCommit/salt/states/users`.

```
veselin:
  user.present:
    - fullname: Veselin Kantsev
    - uid: {{ salt['pillar.get']('users:veselin:uid') }}
    - password: {{ salt['pillar.get']('users:veselin:password') }}
    - groups:
    - wheel
ssh_auth.present:
  - user: veselin
  - source: salt://users/files/veselin.pub
  - require:
  - user: veselin
sudoers:
  file.managed:
    - name: /etc/sudoers.d/wheel
    - contents: '%wheel ALL=(ALL) ALL'
```

We will use YAML to write most Salt configuration. You will notice three different state modules used in the preceding section:

- `user.present`: This module ensures that a given user account exists on the system or creates one if necessary
- `ssh_auth.present`: A module for managing the SSH `authorized_keys` file of a user
- `file.managed`: A module for creating/modifying files

 SaltStack's state modules offer rich functionality. For full details of each module see `https://docs.saltstack.com/en/latest/ref/states/all/`

To avoid hardcoding certain values under `user.present`, we make use of the SaltStack Pillars system. We will examine a pillar file shortly, but for now just note the syntax of referencing pillar values inside our state.

Two other points of interest here are the source of our key file and the `require` property. In this example, a `salt://` formatted source address refers to the Salt File Server which by default serves files from the State Tree (for supported backends, please see `https://docs.saltstack.com/en/latest/ref/file_server/`). The `require` statement enforces an order of execution, ensuring that the user account is present before trying to create an `authorized_keys` file for it.

> SaltStack follows an imperative execution model until such custom ordering is enforced, invoking a declarative mode (see `https://docs.saltstack.com/en/latest/ref/states/ordering.html`).

Thanks to the readability of YAML, one can easily tell what is going on here:

1. We create a new Linux user.
2. We apply desired attributes (uid, password, group, and so on).
3. We deploy an SSH `authorized_keys` file for it.
4. We enable `sudo` for the wheel group of which the user is a member.

Perhaps you could try *edit this state* and *add a user* for yourself? It will be useful later after we deploy.

We will now move on to an NGINX installation via `states/nginx/init.sls`.

> Please refer to: `https://github.com/PacktPublishing/Implementing-D evOps-on-AWS/tree/master/5585_03_CodeFiles/CodeCommit/salt/sta tes/nginx`.

We install NGINX using the `pkg.installed` module:

```
pkg.installed: []
```

Set the service to start on boot (`enable: True`), enable reloading instead of restarting when possible (`reload: True`), ensure the NGINX pkg has been installed (`require:`) before running the service (`service.running:`)

```
nginx:
  service.running:
    - enable: True
    - reload: True
    - require:
      - pkg: nginx
```

Then put a `config` file in place (`file.managed:`), ensuring the service waits for this to happen (`require_in:`) and also reloads each time the file is updated (`watch_in:`):

```
/etc/nginx/conf.d/default.conf:
  file.managed:
    - source: salt://nginx/files/default.conf
    - require:
      - pkg: nginx
    - require_in:
      - service: nginx
    - watch_in:
      - service: nginx
```

Note the `require`/`require_in`, `watch`/`watch_in` pairs. The difference between each of these requisites and its `_in` counterpart lies in the direction in which they act.

For example:

```
nginx:
  service.running:
    - watch:
      - file: nginx_config
nginx_config:
  file.managed:
    - name: /etc/nginx/nginx.conf
    - source: salt://...
```

Has the same effect as:

```
nginx:
  service.running: []
  nginx_config:
  file.managed:
    - name: /etc/nginx/nginx.conf
    - source: salt://...
      - watch_in:
        - service: nginx
```

In both cases, the NGINX service restarts on `config` file changes; however, you can see how the second format can be potentially quite useful the further you get from the service block-say in a different file, as we will see in the next state.

Add in some PHP (`states/php-fpm/init.sls`):

Please refer to:
https://github.com/PacktPublishing/Implementing-DevOps-on-AWS
/tree/master/5585_03_CodeFiles/CodeCommit/salt/states/php-fpm.

```
include:
  - nginx
php-fpm:
  pkg.installed:
    - name: php-fpm
    - require:
      - pkg: nginx
  service.running:
    - name: php-fpm
    - enable: True
    - reload: True
    - require_in:
      - service: nginx...
```

Here you can better see the usefulness of an _in requisite. After we include the nginx state at the top, our require_in makes sure that nginx does not start before php-fpm does.

With NGINX and PHP-FPM now configured, let us add a quick test page (`states/phptest/init.sls`).

Please refer to:
https://github.com/PacktPublishing/Implementing-DevOps-on-AWS
/tree/master/5585_03_CodeFiles/CodeCommit/salt/states/phptest.

We set a few variables pulled from Grains (more on those shortly):

```
{% set publqic_ipv4 = salt['cmd.shell']('ec2-metadata --public-ipv4 | awk
'{ print $2 }'') %}
{% set grains_ipv4 = salt['grains.get']('ipv4:0') %}
{% set grains_os = salt['grains.get']('os') %}
{% set grains_osmajorrelease = salt['grains.get']('osmajorrelease') %}
{% set grains_num_cpus = salt['grains.get']('num_cpus') %}
{% set grains_cpu_model = salt['grains.get']('cpu_model') %}
{% set grains_mem_total = salt['grains.get']('mem_total') %}
```

Then we deploy the test page and add `contents` to it directly:

```
phptest:
  file.managed:
    - name: /var/www/html/index.php
    - makedirs: True
    - contents: |
        <?php
        echo '<p style="text-align:center;color:red">
        Hello from {{ grains_ipv4 }}/{{ public_ipv4 }} running PHP ' .
        phpversion() . ' on {{ grains_os }} {{ grains_osmajorrelease }}.
        <br> I come with {{ grains_num_cpus }} x {{ grains_cpu_model }}
        and {{ grains_mem_total }} MB of memory. </p>';
        phpinfo(INFO_LICENSE);
        ?>
```

We will use this page post-deployment to check whether both NGINX and PHP-FPM are operational.

Pillars

Now let us look at the main mechanism for storing variables in Salt-the Pillars. These are:

- YAML tree-like data structures
- Defined/rendered on the salt-master, unless running masterless in which case they live on the minion
- Useful for storing variables in a central place to be shared by the minions (unless they are masterless)
- Helpful for keeping States portable
- Appropriate for sensitive data (they can also be GPG encrypted; see https://docs.saltstack.com/en/latest/ref/renderers/all/salt.renderers.gpg.html)

We will be using `/srv/salt/pillars` as the root of our Pillar tree on the minion. Let us go back to the `users` state and examine the following lines:

```
- uid: {{ salt['pillar.get']('users:veselin:uid') }}
- password: {{ salt['pillar.get']('users:veselin:password') }}
```

The `uid` and `password` attributes are set to be sourced from a pillar named `users`. And if we check our Pillar Tree, we find a `/srv/salt/pillars/users.sls` file containing:

```
users:
  veselin:
    uid: 5001
    password: '$1$wZ0gQOOo$HEN/gDGS85dEZM7QZVlFz/'
```

It is now easy to see how the `users:veselin:password` reference inside the state file matches against this pillar's structure.

 For more details and examples on pillar usage, see:
https://docs.saltstack.com/en/latest/topics/tutorials/pillar.htm
l

Grains

Unlike Pillars, Grains are considered static data:

- They get generated minion-side and are not shared between different minions
- They contain facts about the minion itself
- Typical examples are CPU, OS, network interfaces, memory, and kernels
- It is possible to add custom Grains to a minion

We have already made good use of Grains within our preceding test page (`states/phptest/init.sls`), getting various host details such as CPU, memory, network, and OS. Another way of using this data is when dealing with multi-OS environments. Let us look at the following example:

```
pkg.installed:
  {% if grains['os'] == 'CentOS' or grains['os'] == 'RedHat' %}
    - name: httpd...
  {% elif grains['os'] == 'Debian' or grains['os'] == 'Ubuntu' %}
    - name: apache2
  ...
  {% endif %}
```

As you see, Grains, much like Pillars, help make our States way more flexible.

Top files

We now have our States ready, even supported by some Pillars and ideally would like to apply all of those to a host so we can get it configured and ready for use.

In SaltStack, the Top File provides the mapping between States/Pillars and the minions they should be applied onto. We have a Top file (`top.sls`) in the root of both the state and pillar trees. We happen to have a single environment (base), but we could easily add more (*dev, qa, prod*). Each could have a separate state and pillar trees with separate Top files which get compiled into one at runtime.

 Please see
`https://docs.saltstack.com/en/latest/ref/states/top.html` for more information on multi-environment setups.

Let us look at a `top.sls` example:

```
base:
  '*':
    - core_utils
    - monitoring_client
      - log_forwarder
  'webserver-*':
    - nginx
    - php-fpm
  'dbserver-*':
    - pgsql_server
    - pgbouncer
```

We are declaring that in our base (default) environment:

- All minions should have the core set of utilities, the monitoring and log forwarding agents installed
- Minions with an ID matching `webserver-*`, get the `nginx` and `php-fpm` States (in addition to the previous three)
- Database nodes get applied: the common three plus `pgsql_server` and `pgbouncer`

Minion targeting gets even more interesting when you include Pillars, Grains, or a mix of these (see
`https://docs.saltstack.com/en/latest/ref/states/top.html#advanced-minion-targeting`).

By specifying such state/pillar to a minion association, from a security standpoint we also create a useful isolation. Say our Pillars contained sensitive data, then this is how we could limit the group of minions who are allowed access to it.

Back to our Salt repository, where we find two `top.sls` files:

- `salt/states/top.sls`:

```
base:
  '*':
    - users
    - nginx
    - php-fpm
    - phptest
```

- `salt/pillars/top.sls`:

```
base:
  '*':
    - users
```

We can allow ourselves to target *, as we are running in masterless mode and essentially all our States/Pillars are intended for the local minion.

We enable this mode with a few settings in a minion configuration file (`/etc/salt/minion.d/masterless.conf`).

> Please refer to:
> `https://github.com/PacktPublishing/Implementing-DevOps-on-AWS`
> `/blob/master/5585_03_CodeFiles/CodeCommit/salt/minion.d/master`
> `less.conf`.

These effectively tell the salt-minion process that the Salt Fileserver, the state tree and the pillar tree are all to be found on the local filesystem. You will see how this configuration file gets deployed via UserData in a moment.

> More on running masterless can be found at:
> `https://docs.saltstack.com/en/latest/topics/tutorials/standalone`
> `_minion.html`

This concludes our SaltStack internals session. As you get more comfortable, you may want to look into Salt Engines, Beacons, writing your own modules and/or Salt Formulas. And those are only some of the ninja features being constantly added to the project.

At this stage we already know how to use Terraform to deploy and now SaltStack to configure.

Bootstrapping nodes under Configuration Management (end-to-end IaC)

Without further delay, let us get our old VPC re-deployed along with a configuration-managed web service inside it.

Terraform will spawn the VPC, ELB, and EC2 nodes then bootstrap the SaltStack workflow with the use of EC2 UserData. Naturally, we strive to reuse as much code as possible; however, our next deployment requires some changes to the TF templates.

Please refer to:
`https://github.com/PacktPublishing/Implementing-DevOps-on-AWS`
`/tree/master/5585_03_CodeFiles/Terraform`.

`resources.tf`:

- We do not need the private subnets/route tables, NAT, nor RDS resources this time, so we have removed these, making the deployment a bit faster.
- We will be using an IAM Role to grant permission to the EC2 node to access the CodeCommit repository.
    - We have declared the role:

```
resource "aws_iam_role" "terraform-role" {
name = "terraform-role"path = "/"...
```

    - We have added and associated a policy (granting read access to CodeCommit) with that role:

```
resource "aws_iam_role_policy" "terraform-policy" {
name = "terraform-policy"
role = "${aws_iam_role.terraform-role.id}"...
```

    - We have created and associated an instance profile with the role:

```
resource "aws_iam_instance_profile" "terraform-profile" {
name = "terraform-profile"
roles = ["${aws_iam_role.terraform-role.name}"]
...
```

- We have updated the Auto Scaling launch-configuration with the instance profile ID:

```
resource "aws_launch_configuration" "terraform-lcfg"
{...iam_instance_profile =
"${aws_iam_instance_profile.terraform-profile.id}"
    . . .
```

- We have updated the UserData script with some SaltStack bootstrap instructions, to install Git and SaltStack, checkout and put our Salt code in place and finally run Salt:

```
user_data = <<EOF
#!/bin/bash
set -euf -o pipefail
exec 1> >(logger -s -t $(basename $0)) 2>&1
# Install Git and set CodeComit connection settings
# (required for access via IAM roles)
yum -y install git
git config --system credential.helper
'!aws codecommit credential-helper $@'
git config --system credential.UseHttpPath true
# Clone the Salt repository
git clone https://git-codecommit.us-east-1.amazonaws.com/v1/repos/
salt/srv/salt; chmod 700 /srv/salt
# Install SaltStack
yum -y install https://repo.saltstack.com/yum/amazon/
salt-amzn-repo-latest-1.ami.noarch.rpm
yum clean expire-cache; yum -y install salt-minion;
chkconfig salt-minion off
# Put custom minion config in place (for enabling masterless mode)
cp -r /srv/salt/minion.d /etc/salt/
# Trigger a full Salt run
salt-call state.apply
EOF
We have moved our EC2 node (the Auto Scaling group)
to a public subnet and allowed incoming SSH traffic
so that we can connect and play with Salt on it:
resource "aws_security_group" "terraform-ec2" {ingress {
from_port = "22"
to_port = "22"
...resource "aws_autoscaling_group" "terraform-asg" {
. . .
vpc_zone_identifier = ["${aws_subnet.public-1.id}",
. . .
```

variables.tf:

We have removed all RDS related variables.

`outputs.tf`:

We have removed RDS and NAT related outputs.

`iam_user_policy.json`:

This document will become useful shortly as we will need to create a new user for the deployment. We have removed RDS permissions and added IAM ones from it.

We are now ready for deployment. Pre-flight check:

- Updated Terraform templates

 Please refer to: `https://github.com/PacktPublishing/Implementing-D evOps-on-AWS/tree/master/5585_03_CodeFiles/Terraform`) are available locally in our designated terraform folder

- Created/updated our Terraform IAM account with the new set of permissions as per `iam_user_policy.json`
- Ensured we have a copy of the `terraform ec2 keypair` (for SSH-ing later)
- All our SaltStack code has been pushed up to the Salt CodeCommit repository (Please refer to:
  `https://git-codecommit.us-east-1.amazonaws.com/v1/repos/salt`)

Let us export our credentials and launch Terraform:

```
$ export AWS_ACCESS_KEY_ID='user_access_key'
$ export AWS_SECRET_ACCESS_KEY='user_secret_access_key'
$ export AWS_DEFAULT_REGION='us-east-1'$ cd Terraform/$ terraform
validate
$ terraform plan...Plan: 15 to add, 0 to change, 0 to destroy.
$ terraform apply...Outputs:
ELB URI = terraform-elb-xxxxxx.us-east-1.elb.amazonaws.com
VPC ID = vpc-xxxxxx
```

Allow 3-5 minutes for output `t2.nano` to come into shape and then browse to the ELB URI from the following output:

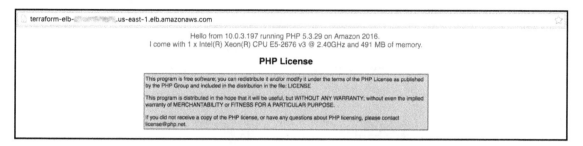

Victory!

Try increasing the *autoscaling-group-minsize* and *autoscaling-group-maxsize* in `terraform.tfvars`, then re-applying the template. You should start seeing different IPs when the page is refreshed.

Given the preceding test page, we can be reasonably confident that Salt bootstrapped and applied our set of States successfully.

We did, however, enable SSH access in order to be able to experiment more with Salt, so let us do that.

We see the public IP of the node on our test page. You could SSH into it with either the `terraform ec2 keypair` or the default `ec2-user` Linux account, or if you dared create one for yourself in the `users/init.sls` state earlier, you could use it now.

Once connected, we can use the `salt-call` command (as root) to interact with Salt locally:

- How about some Pillars:

```
# salt-call pillar.items
```

- Or let us see what Grains we have:

```
# salt-call grains.items
```

- Run individual States:

```
# salt-call state.apply nginx
```

- Or execute a full run, that is of all assigned States as per the Top file:

```
# salt-call state.apply
```

After playing with our new deployment for a bit, I suspect you are going to want to try adding or changing States/Pillars or other parts of the Salt code. As per the IaC rules we agreed upon earlier, every change we make goes through Git, but let us examine what options we have for deploying those changes afterwards:

- Pull the changes down to each minion and run `salt-call`
- Provision new minions which will pull down the latest code
- Push changes via a Salt-master

It is easy to see that the first option will work with the couple of nodes we use for testing, but is quickly going to become hard to manage at scale.

Provisioning new minions on each deployment is a valid option if masterless Salt setup is preferred; however, you need to consider the frequency of deployments in your environment and the associated cost of replacing EC2 nodes. One benefit worth nothing here is that of blue/green deployments. By provisioning new minions to serve your code changes, you get to keep the old ones around for a while which allows you to shift traffic gradually and roll back safely if needed.

Having a Salt-master would be my recommended approach for any non-dev environments. The Salt code is kept on it, so any Git changes you make, need to be pulled down only once. You can then deploy the changed States/Pillars by targeting the minions you want from the Salt-master. You could still do blue/green for major releases or you could choose to deploy to your current minions directly if it is just a minor, safe amendment, or perhaps something critical that needs to reach all minions as soon as possible.

Another powerful feature of the Salt-master is orchestration, more specifically-remote execution. With all your minions connected to it, the salt-master becomes a command center from which you have more or less full control over them.

Executing commands on the minions is done via modules from generic ones such as `cmd.run`, which essentially allows you to run arbitrary shell commands to more specialized ones such as `nginx`, `postfix`, `selinux`, or `zfs`. The list is quite long as you can see here: `https://docs.saltstack.com/en/latest/ref/modules/all/index.html`.

And if you recall the earlier section on hostnames and naming conventions, this is where one can appreciate their value. It is quite convenient to be able to execute statements like:

```
salt 'webserver-*' nginx.status
salt 'db-*' postgres.db_list
```

You can also use Pillars and/or Grains to add tags to your hosts, so you could further group them per location, role, department, or something similar.

In brief, here are a few key points of masterless versus a salt-master arrangement:

Salt Master	Masterless
• A powerful, centralized control platform (must be secured adequately) which allows for quick, parallel access to a vast network of minions • Advanced features such as Salt Engines, Runners, Beacons, the Reactor System • API access	• No salt-master node to maintain • Not having a single node which provides full access to the rest of them is more secure in some sense • Simpler Salt operation • After the initial Salt execution, the minions can be considered immutable

For many *FOR LOOP gurus* out there, parallel execution tools like Salt are very appealing. It allows you to rapidly reach out to nodes at a massive scale, whether you simply want to query their uptime, reload a service, or react to a threat alert by stopping sshd across your cluster.

 Before you go, please remember to delete any AWS resources used in the preceding examples (VPC, ELB, EC2, IAM, CodeCommit, and so on) to avoid unexpected charges.

Summary

In this chapter, we examined the second part of *Infrastructure as Code*, namely **Configuration Management**.

We learned about a few different components of the CM solution SaltStack: States, Pillars, Grains, and the Top File. We learned how to use them and how to write code for them.

We then combined our previous knowledge of how to deploy infrastructure using Terraform with that of how to configure it using SaltStack, resulting in our first end-to-end IaC deployment.

Next, we are going to look into *Continuous Integration*: what it is and how to setup a *CI* pipeline on AWS.

4
Build, Test, and Release Faster with Continuous Integration

The emphasis of this chapter will be the value of quick iteration: Quick over quality iteration, as per Boyd's law (you might recall the OODA principle mentioned in `Chapter 1`, *What Is DevOps and Should You Care?*).

By iteration, I am referring to a software development cycle, from the moment a piece of code is written, published (committed to version control), compiled (if needed), tested and finally deployed.

Continuous Integration (**CI**) defines the routines that should be adopted by developers plus the necessary tools to make this iteration as fast as possible.

Let us start with the human factor:

- Use version control (for example Git)
- Commit smaller changes, more often
- Test locally first
- Do peer code reviews
- Pause other team activity until an issue is resolved

Then add a bit of automation (a CI server):

- Monitor for version control changes (for example Git commits)
- Pull down changed code
- Compile and run tests
    - On success, build an artefact
    - On failure, notify the team and pause the pipeline
- Repeat

Committing smaller changes helps detect problems earlier and potentially solves them much more easily; and a developer receives feedback on their work more frequently which builds confidence that their code is in a good state.

Testing locally, where possible, greatly reduces team distraction caused by the CI pipeline tripping over minor issues.

Code reviews are beneficial at many levels. They eliminate bad coding habits as peers ensure code complies with agreed standards. They increase visibility; peers get a lot more exposure to the work of others. They help catch the errors which a machine would miss.

The **Toyota Way** teaches us to *Stop the Line* whenever a problem is detected. In terms of CI, this translates into halting the pipeline on errors and concentrating resources on fixing these. At first this might seem like an obvious way to reduce productivity and slow down the whole process, but it's been proven again and again that the initial overhead is ultimately worth it. This way you keep your technical debt to a minimum; improve code as-you-go, preventing issues from accumulating and re-surfacing at a later stage. Now is a good time to restate the **test locally** point made earlier. You would likely not want to interrupt your colleagues with something trivial, which could have been spotted easily before committing.

As you succeed in building this team discipline (the hard part), it is time to add some automation flavor by setting up a CI pipeline.

The CI server tirelessly monitors your code repository and reacts to changes by performing a set of tasks over and over again. I believe it is evident how this saves engineers a great amount of time and effort, not to mention the fact that they avoid having to address the monotone nature of such work.

A pipeline, say in Jenkins, would normally consist of a number of stages: individual stages can represent the checking out of the latest code, running build tasks on it, performing tests then building artefacts, where each stage runs subject to the previous one completing successfully.

This generally describes how a combination of engineer habits and some tooling can greatly improve a software development cycle. Continuous Integration helps us collaborate better, write better code, ship more often and get feedback quicker.

Users want new features released fast, developers want to see the result of their work out there – everybody wins.

We have discussed the theory, now let us bring our focus to the title of this chapter. We are going to use our acquired Terraform and Salt skills to deploy a CI environment on AWS featuring a Jenkins (v2) CI server.

Jenkins (ref: `https://jenkins.io`) is a popular, well established open source project focusing on automation. It comes with a long list of integrations, catering to a variety of platforms and programming languages. Meet Jenkins:
`https://wiki.jenkins-ci.org/display/JENKINS/Meet+Jenkins`.

The deployment of our CI environment can be broken down into three main stages:

1. Prepare an **Infrastructure as Code** deployment:

    - Write **Terraform** templates to provision a VPC and an EC2 instance
    - Write **Salt** States to install Jenkins, NGINX and other software onto the EC2 instance

2. Deploy IaC:

    - Deploy the Terraform templates and Salt States

3. Setup CI:

    - Configure a Jenkins pipeline for Continuous Integration of a demo application

Prepare IaC

In accordance with our *Infrastructure as Code* principles, this deployment will also be mostly template driven. We will try to reuse some of the Terraform and Salt code from previous chapters.

Terraform templates

For this particular setup we can simplify our template as we will only need the VPC, some networking bits, and an EC2 instance.

Let's browse through the files in our *TF* repository:

 Please refer to:
https://github.com/PacktPublishing/Implementing-DevOps-on-AWS
/blob/master/5585_04_CodeFiles/Terraform/variables.tf.

Variables

The few variables we need can be grouped into VPC and EC2 related ones:

VPC

```
variable "aws-region" {
  type = "string"
  description = "AWS region"
}
variable "vpc-cidr" {
  type = "string"
  description = "VPC CIDR"
}
variable "vpc-name" {
  type = "string"
  description = "VPC name"
}
variable "aws-availability-zones" {
  type = "string"
  description = "AWS zones"
}
```

EC2

```
variable "jenkins-ami-id" {
  type="string"
  description = "EC2 AMI identifier"
}
variable "jenkins-instance-type" {
  type = "string"
  description = "EC2 instance type"
}
variable "jenkins-key-name" {
```

```
    type = "string"
    description = "EC2 ssh key name"
}
```

Variables (values)

Following the bare variable definitions, we now supply some values:

 Please refer to:
https://github.com/PacktPublishing/Implementing-DevOps-on-AWS
/blob/master/5585_04_CodeFiles/Terraform/terraform.tfvars.

VPC

We'll keep our deployment in US East:

```
aws-region = "us-east-1"
vpc-cidr = "10.0.0.0/16"
vpc-name = "Terraform"
aws-availability-zones = "us-east-1b,us-east-1c"
```

EC2

A Nano instance will be sufficient for testing. Ensure the referenced key-pair exists:

```
jenkins-ami-id = "ami-6869aa05"
jenkins-instance-type = "t2.nano"
jenkins-key-name = "terraform"
```

Resources

 Please refer to:
https://github.com/PacktPublishing/Implementing-DevOps-on-AWS
/blob/master/5585_04_CodeFiles/Terraform/resources.tf.

Create the VPC

As a matter of standard (good) practice we create all our resources inside a VPC:

```
# Set a Provider
provider "aws" {
  region = "${var.aws-region}"
```

```
}

# Create a VPC
resource "aws_vpc" "terraform-vpc" {
  cidr_block = "${var.vpc-cidr}"

  tags {
    Name = "${var.vpc-name}"
  }
}
```

Add networking components

We add a gateway, a route table, and an Internet facing subnet from where our Jenkins instance will be launched:

IGW

```
# Create an Internet Gateway
resource "aws_internet_gateway" "terraform-igw" {
  vpc_id = "${aws_vpc.terraform-vpc.id}"
}
```

Route table

```
# Create public route tables
resource "aws_route_table" "public" {
  vpc_id = "${aws_vpc.terraform-vpc.id}"
  route {
    cidr_block = "0.0.0.0/0"
    gateway_id = "${aws_internet_gateway.terraform-igw.id}"
  }

  tags {
    Name = "Public"
  }
}
```

Subnet

```
# Create and associate public subnets with a route table
resource "aws_subnet" "public-1" {
  vpc_id = "${aws_vpc.terraform-vpc.id}"
  cidr_block = "${cidrsubnet(var.vpc-cidr, 8, 1)}"
  availability_zone = "${element(split(",",var.aws-availability-zones),
count.index)}"
  map_public_ip_on_launch = true
```

```
  tags {
    Name = "Public"
  }
}

resource "aws_route_table_association" "public-1" {
  subnet_id = "${aws_subnet.public-1.id}"
  route_table_id = "${aws_route_table.public.id}"
}
```

Add EC2 node and related resources

The security group for our Jenkins node needs to permit HTTP/S access plus SSH for convenience, so that we can access the command line if needed:

Security Group

```
resource "aws_security_group" "jenkins" {
  name = "jenkins"
  description = "ec2 instance security group"
  vpc_id = "${aws_vpc.terraform-vpc.id}"

  ingress {
    from_port = "22"
    to_port = "22"
    protocol = "tcp"
    cidr_blocks = ["0.0.0.0/0"]
  }

  ingress {
    from_port = "80"
    to_port = "80"
    protocol = "tcp"
    cidr_blocks = ["0.0.0.0/0"]
  }

  ingress {
    from_port = "443"
    to_port = "443"
    protocol = "tcp"
    cidr_blocks = ["0.0.0.0/0"]
  }

  egress {
    from_port = 0
    to_port = 0
    protocol = "-1"
```

```
    cidr_blocks = ["0.0.0.0/0"]
  }

}
```

IAM Role

We will use an IAM Role to grant Jenkins access to AWS services:

```
resource "aws_iam_role" "jenkins" {
    name = "jenkins"
    path = "/"
    assume_role_policy = <<EOF
{
  "Version": "2012-10-17",
  "Statement": [
    {
      "Action": "sts:AssumeRole",
      "Principal": {
        "Service": "ec2.amazonaws.com"
      },
      "Effect": "Allow",
      "Sid": ""
    }
  ]
}
EOF
}
```

IAM Role Policy

This policy will allow Jenkins to read from a codecommit repository and perform all actions (except deleting) on an s3 bucket:

```
resource "aws_iam_role_policy" "jenkins" {
    name = "jenkins"
    role = "${aws_iam_role.jenkins.id}"
    policy = <<EOF
{
    "Version": "2012-10-17",
    "Statement": [
        {
            "Effect": "Allow",
            "Action": [
                "codecommit:Get*",
                "codecommit:GitPull",
                "codecommit:List*"
            ],
```

```
            "Resource": "*"
        },
        {
            "Effect": "Allow",
            "NotAction": [
                "s3:DeleteBucket"
            ],
            "Resource": "*"
        }
    ]
}
EOF
}
```

IAM Profile

```
resource "aws_iam_instance_profile" "jenkins" {
    name = "jenkins"
    roles = ["${aws_iam_role.jenkins.name}"]
}
```

EC2 instance

Here we define a single instance along with its bootstrap UserData script:

```
resource "aws_instance" "jenkins" {
    ami = "${var.jenkins-ami-id}"
    instance_type = "${var.jenkins-instance-type}"
    key_name = "${var.jenkins-key-name}"
    vpc_security_group_ids = ["${aws_security_group.jenkins.id}"]
    iam_instance_profile = "${aws_iam_instance_profile.jenkins.id}"
    subnet_id = "${aws_subnet.public-1.id}"
    tags { Name = "jenkins" }
```

Here we set the attributes needed to launch an EC2 instance, such as the instance type, the AMI to be used, security group(s), subnet and so on.

Next, we add the bootstrap shell script to help us install required packages, checkout Git repositories and run Salt:

```
    user_data = <<EOF
#!/bin/bash
set -euf -o pipefail
exec 1> >(logger -s -t $(basename $0)) 2>&1
# Install Git and set CodeComit connection settings
# (required for access via IAM roles)
yum -y install git
```

```
git config --system credential.helper '!aws codecommit credential-helper
$@'
git config --system credential.UseHttpPath true
# Clone the Salt repository
git clone https://git-codecommit.us-east-1.amazonaws.com/v1/repos/salt
/srv/salt; chmod 700 /srv/salt
# Install SaltStack
yum -y install
https://repo.saltstack.com/yum/amazon/salt-amzn-repo-latest-1.ami.noarch.rp
m
yum clean expire-cache; yum -y install salt-minion; chkconfig salt-minion
off
# Put custom minion config in place (for enabling masterless mode)
cp -r /srv/salt/minion.d /etc/salt/
# Trigger a full Salt run
salt-call state.apply
EOF

    lifecycle { create_before_destroy = true }
}
```

Elastic IP

Finally, we provision a static IP for Jenkins:

```
resource "aws_eip" "jenkins" {
  instance = "${aws_instance.jenkins.id}"
  vpc      = true
}
```

Outputs

 Please refer to:
https://github.com/PacktPublishing/Implementing-DevOps-on-AWS
/blob/master/5585_04_CodeFiles/Terraform/outputs.tf.

Some useful outputs to provide us with the address of the Jenkins node:

```
output "VPC ID" {
  value = "${aws_vpc.terraform-vpc.id}"
}

output "JENKINS EIP" {
  value = "${aws_eip.jenkins.public_ip}"
}
```

And that is our VPC infrastructure defined. Now we can move onto Salt and the application stack.

SaltStack code

You'll remember our favorite Configuration Management tool from the previous chapter. We will use SaltStack to configure the EC2 Jenkins node for us.

States

 Please refer to:
https://github.com/PacktPublishing/Implementing-DevOps-on-AWS
/tree/master/5585_04_CodeFiles/CodeCommit/salt/states.

top.sls

We are working with a single minion, and all our states apply to it:

```
base:
  '*':
    - users
    - yum-s3
    - jenkins
    - nginx
    - docker
```

users

We add a Linux user account, configure its SSH keys and **sudo** access:

```
veselin:
  user.present:
    - fullname: Veselin Kantsev
    - uid: {{ salt['pillar.get']('users:veselin:uid') }}
  ...
```

yum-s3

As part of our CI pipeline, we will be storing RPM artefacts in S3. Cob (ref: https://github.com/henrysher/cob) is a Yum package manager plugin which makes it possible to access S3 based RPM repositories using an IAM Role.

We deploy the plugin, its configuration and a repository definition (disabled for now) as managed files:

```
yum-s3_cob.py:
  file.managed:
    - name: /usr/lib/yum-plugins/cob.py
    - source: salt://yum-s3/files/cob.py

yum-s3_cob.conf:
  file.managed:
    - name: /etc/yum/pluginconf.d/cob.conf
    - source: salt://yum-s3/files/cob.conf

yum-s3_s3.repo:
  file.managed:
    - name: /etc/yum.repos.d/s3.repo
    - source: salt://yum-s3/files/s3.repo
```

Jenkins

Here comes the lead character – Mr Jenkins. We make use of Docker in our CI pipeline, hence the `include` following. Docker allows us to run the different pipeline steps in isolation, which makes dependency management much easier and helps keeps the Jenkins node clean.

```
include:
  - docker
```

Also we ensure Java and a few other prerequisites get installed:

```
jenkins_prereq:
  pkg.installed:
    - pkgs:
      - java-1.7.0-openjdk
      - gcc
      - make
      - createrepo
```

Then, install Jenkins itself:

```
jenkins:
  pkg.installed:
    - sources:
      - jenkins:
http://mirrors.jenkins-ci.org/redhat-stable/jenkins-2.7.1-1.1.noarch.rpm
    - require:
      - pkg: jenkins_prereq
  ...
```

NGINX

We will use NGINX as a reverse proxy and an SSL termination point. That is not to say that Jenkins cannot serve on its own, it is just considered better practice to separate the roles:

```
include:
  - jenkins

nginx:
  pkg.installed: []
...
{% for FIL in ['crt','key'] %}
/etc/nginx/ssl/server.{{ FIL }}:
...
{% endfor %}
```

Docker

It is about time we mentioned Docker, given its (deserved) popularity nowadays. It is very well suited to our CI needs, providing isolated environments for the various tests and builds that may be required:

```
docker:
  pkg.installed: []

  service.running:
    - enable: True
    - reload: True
```

Pillars

 Please refer to:
https://github.com/PacktPublishing/Implementing-DevOps-on-AWS
/tree/master/5585_04_CodeFiles/CodeCommit/salt/pillars.

top.sls

Our standalone minion gets it all:

```
base:
  '*':
    - users
    - nginx
```

users

Setting a password hash and a consistent UID for the Linux account:

```
users:
  veselin:
    uid: 5001
    password: ...
```

NGINX

We store the SSL data in this Pillar:

```
nginx:
  crt: |
    -----BEGIN CERTIFICATE-----
    ...
    -----END CERTIFICATE-----
  key: |
    -----BEGIN RSA PRIVATE KEY-----
    ...
    -----END RSA PRIVATE KEY-----
```

Minion configuration

Please refer to:
`https://github.com/PacktPublishing/Implementing-DevOps-on-AWS`
`/tree/master/5585_04_CodeFiles/CodeCommit/salt/minion.d.`

masterless.conf

We are still using Salt in standalone (masterless) mode, so this is our extra `minion` configuration:

```
file_client: local
file_roots:
  base:
    - /srv/salt/states
pillar_roots:
  base:
    - /srv/salt/pillars
```

Thanks to all of the preceding codes, we should be able to run Terraform and end up with a Jenkins service ready for use.

Let us give that a try.

Deploy IaC

We start by creating a Terraform EC2 key-pair and a Terraform IAM user as in previous chapters (do not forget to write down access/secret API keys). Then we grant permissions to the IAM user to perform actions with the EC2, IAM, S3 and CodeCommit services:

 Please refer to:
https://github.com/PacktPublishing/Implementing-DevOps-on-AWS
/blob/master/5585_04_CodeFiles/Terraform/iam_user_policy.json.

```
{
    "Version": "2012-10-17",
    "Statement": [
        {
            "Effect": "Allow",
            "NotAction": [
                "codecommit:DeleteRepository"
            ],
            "Resource": "*"
        },
        {
            "Effect": "Allow",
            "NotAction": [
                "s3:DeleteBucket"
            ],
            "Resource": "*"
        },
        {
            "Sid": "Stmt1461764665000",
            "Effect": "Allow",
            "Action": [
                "ec2:AllocateAddress",
    ...
```

Then we associate a SSH public key with the user (as per the screenshots in the previous chapter) to allow `codecommit` repository access.

Next, we need to setup our AWS CLI environment with the keys we produced earlier:

```
$ export AWS_ACCESS_KEY_ID='user_access_key'
$ export AWS_SECRET_ACCESS_KEY='user_secret_access_key'
$ export AWS_DEFAULT_REGION='us-east-1'
```

Now we should be able to use the CLI tool and create our SaltStack repository:

```
$ aws codecommit create-repository --repository-name salt
  --repository-description "SaltStack repo"
{
"repositoryMetadata": {
"repositoryName": "salt",
"cloneUrlSsh":
"ssh://git-codecommit.us-east-1.amazonaws.com/v1/repos/salt",
...
```

We clone the repository locally:

```
$ git clone ssh://SSH_KEY_ID@git-codecommit.us-east-
  1.amazonaws.com/v1/repos/salt
Cloning into 'salt'...
warning: You appear to have cloned an empty repository.
Checking connectivity... done.
```

(where SSH_KEY_ID is the one we saw after uploading a public key here)

Finally, you can copy the ready salt code examples for this chapter, commit and push to the codecommit repository.

Please refer to:
https://github.com/PacktPublishing/Implementing-DevOps-on-AWS
/tree/master/5585_04_CodeFiles/CodeCommit/salt

With the SaltStack repo in sync, we can proceed with Terraform and the bootstrap process. Inside our TF templates folder we run the familiar command sequence:

```
$ terraform validate
$ terraform plan
Refreshing Terraform state prior to plan...
...
Plan: 11 to add, 0 to change, 0 to destroy.
$ terraform apply
aws_iam_role.jenkins: Creating...
...
Apply complete! Resources: 11 added, 0 changed, 0 destroyed.
Outputs:
   JENKINS EIP = x.x.x.x
   VPC ID      = vpc-xxxxxx
```

At the end we get the IP of our Jenkins node which we would need to resolve into a hostname (for example via the `nslookup` cmd). Load that in your browser and you should be greeted by Jenkins.

Setup CI

After a successful Terraform deployment, it is time to move onto service configuration. More specifically, Jenkins and the integration pipeline.

Jenkins initialization

With Jenkins running for the first time, we need to complete a short setup routine. First, we need to SSH into the node and retrieve the admin password stored in `/var/lib/jenkins/secrets/initialAdminPassword`:

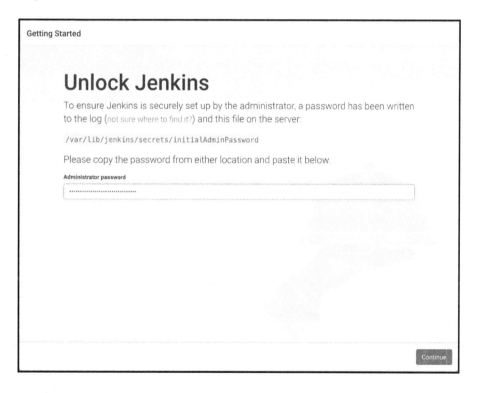

We are mainly interested in the pipeline group of plugins which is included with the suggested ones:

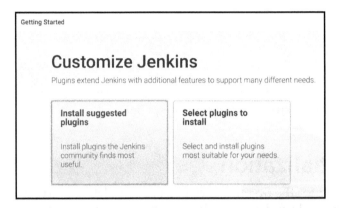

After the plugins installation has completed, it's time to create our first user:

With this the initialization process is complete and Jenkins is ready for use:

Writing a demo app

Before configuring the CI pipeline, it will help to have something to do some integration on. A basic Hello World type of PHP code will do, so with a sincere apology to all PHP developers out there, I present you with the source of our demo app:

> Please refer to:
> https://github.com/PacktPublishing/Implementing-DevOps-on-AWS/tree/master/5585_04_CodeFiles/CodeCommit/demo-app.

```
src/index.php:
<?php

function greet($name) {
  return "Hello $name!";
}

$full_name = "Bobby D";
 greet ($full_name);

Clapping fades...
And naturally, a unit test for it:
tests/indexTest.php:

<?php
require_once "src/index.php";

class IndexTest extends PHPUnit_Framework_TestCase
{
  public function testGreet() {
    global $full_name;
    $expected = "Hello $full_name!";
```

```
    $actual = greet($full_name);
    $this->assertEquals($expected, $actual);
    }
}
```

There is a third file in our `demo-app` folder curiously named `Jenkinsfile` which we will discuss shortly.

Now let us get our code into a repository:

```
$ aws codecommit create-repository --repository-name demo-app
  --repository-description "Demo app"
{
"repositoryMetadata": {
"repositoryName": "demo-app",
"cloneUrlSsh":
"ssh://git-codecommit.us-east-1.amazonaws.com/v1/repos/demo-app"
. . .
Then we clone it locally (replace SSH_KEY_ID as before):
$ git clone ssh://SSH_KEY_ID@git-codecommit.us-east-
  1.amazonaws.com/v1/repos/demo-app
. . .
```

Finally, we place our `demo-app` code into the empty repository, commit and push all changes to codecommit.

Defining the pipeline

It is time to decide on what the CI pipeline is meant to do for us. Here is a list of useful steps as a start:

1. Checkout application source code from Git
2. Run tests against it by running PHPUnit inside a Docker container (on the Jenkins host)
3. Build application artefacts by executing FPM within a container on the Jenkins host
4. Upload artefacts to an external store (for example, a Yum repository)

Translated into Jenkins pipeline code:

Please refer to:
https://github.com/PacktPublishing/Implementing-DevOps-on-AWS
/blob/master/5585_04_CodeFiles/CodeCommit/demo-app/Jenkinsfile.

```groovy
#!groovy

node {

  stage "Checkout Git repo"
    checkout scm
  stage "Run tests"
    sh "docker run -v \$(pwd):/app --rm phpunit/phpunit tests/"
  stage "Build RPM"
    sh "[ -d ./rpm ] || mkdir ./rpm"
    sh "docker run -v \$(pwd)/src:/data/demo-app -v \$(pwd)/rpm:/data/rpm -
-rm tenzer/fpm fpm -s dir -t rpm -n demo-app -v \$(git rev-parse --short
HEAD) --description "Demo PHP app" --directories /var/www/demo-app --
package /data/rpm/demo-app-\$(git rev-parse --short HEAD).rpm /data/demo-
app=/var/www/"

  stage "Update YUM repo"
    sh "[ -d ~/repo/rpm/demo-app/ ] || mkdir -p ~/repo/rpm/demo-app/"
    sh "mv ./rpm/*.rpm ~/repo/rpm/demo-app/"
    sh "createrepo ~/repo/"
    sh "aws s3 sync ~/repo s3://MY_BUCKET_NAME/ --region us-east-1 --
delete"

  stage "Check YUM repo"
    sh "yum clean all"
    sh "yum info demo-app-\$(git rev-parse --short HEAD)"
}
```

Generally speaking, defining a pipeline consists of a setting out a series of tasks/stages. Let us review each of the preceding stages:

- We start with a Git checkout of our demo-app code. The repository address is assumed to be the one of the Jenkinsfile.

- At the next stage we take advantage of Docker's isolation and spin up a container with everything needed for PHPUnit (ref: https://phpunit.de) to run a test against our demo-app source code. Take a look in the tests/ folder under ${GIT_URL}/Examples/Chapter-4/CodeCommit/demo-app/ if you would like to add more or modify it further.

- If the tests pass, we move onto building an RPM artefact using a neat, user-friendly tool called FPM (ref: https://github.com/jordansissel/fpm), again in a Docker container. We use the short git commit hash as the version identifier for our demo-app.

- We move our RPM artefact to a designated repository folder, create a YUM repository out of it using `createrepo` and sync all that data to an Amazon S3 bucket. The idea is to use this S3 based YUM repository later on for deploying our `demo-app`.
- Finally, as a bonus, we check that the package we just synced can be retrieved via YUM.

Our pipeline is now defined but before we can run it, we need to satisfy one (S3) dependency. We need to create a S3 bucket to store the RPM artefacts that the pipeline would produce. Then we need to update parts of the Jenkins and Saltstack code with the address of that S3 bucket.

To interact with S3, we shall use the AWS CLI tool within the environment we configured for Terraform earlier:

```
$ aws s3 mb s3://MY_BUCKET_NAME
```

The bucket name is up to you, but keep in mind that the global S3 namespace is shared, so the more unique the name the better.

Next, we update our pipeline definition (`Jenkinsfile`). Look for the line containing `MY_BUCKET_NAME`:

```
sh "aws s3 sync ~/repo s3://MY_BUCKET_NAME/ --region us-east-1
    --delete"
```

We also need to update SaltStack (again replacing `MY_BUCKET_NAME`):

Please refer to:
https://github.com/PacktPublishing/Implementing-DevOps-on-AWS
/blob/master/5585_04_CodeFiles/CodeCommit/salt/states/yum-s3/f
iles/s3.repo.

```
[s3-repo]
name=S3-repo
baseurl=https://s3.amazonaws.com/MY_BUCKET_NAME
enabled=1
gpgcheck=0
```

This `repo` file will be used in the last stage of our pipeline, as we will see in a moment. At this point you will need to commit and push both changes: the `Jenkinsfile` to the `demo-app` repository and the `s3.repo` file to the SaltStack one. Then you would SSH into the Jenkins node, pull and apply the Salt changes.

Setting up the pipeline

Back to the Jenkins interface. After logging in, we click on the `create new jobs` link on the welcome page:

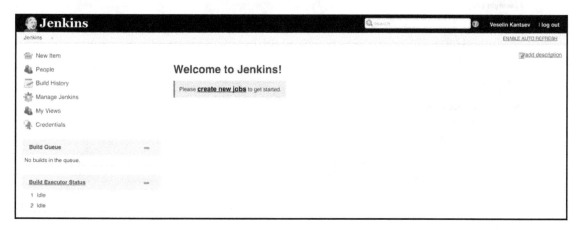

We select **Pipeline** as a job type and pick a name for it:

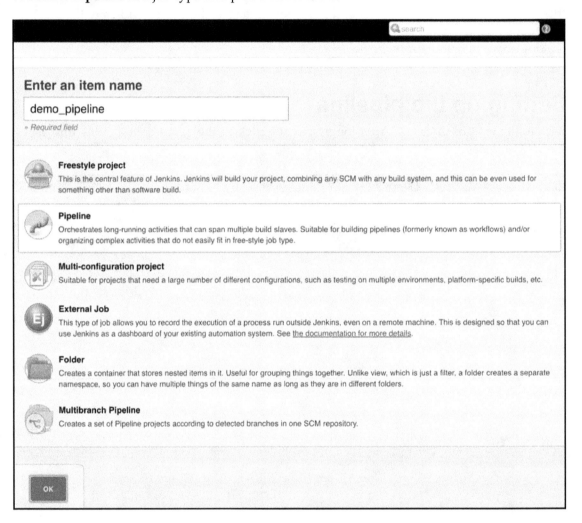

The next screen takes us to the job configuration details. At the top we choose to **Discard old builds** in order to keep our Jenkins workspace compact. We are saying, only keep details of the last five executions of this job:

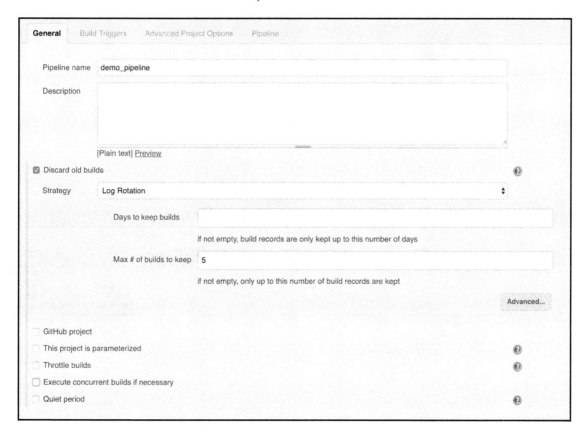

Under **Build Triggers** we choose to poll our Git repository for changes every 5 minutes:

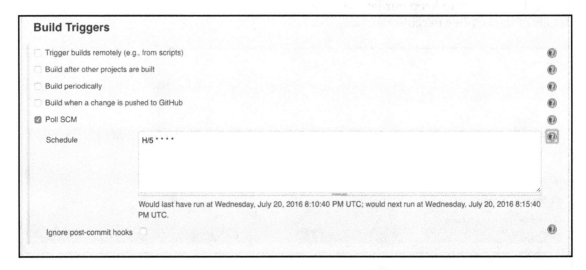

Underneath, we choose **Pipeline script from SCM**, set SCM to **Git** and add the URL of our `demo-app` repository (that is
`https://git-codecommit.us-east-1.amazonaws.com/v1/repos/demo-app`) to be polled:

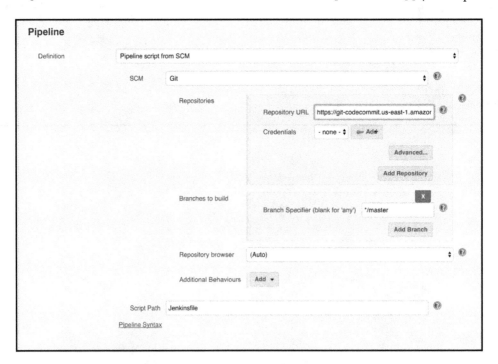

No need for extra credentials as these will be fetched via the EC2 IAM Role. Note the **Script Path** referencing the Jenkins file we mentioned earlier. This is a great new feature which gives us pipeline as code functionality as described here:

`https://jenkins.io/doc/pipeline/#loading-pipeline-scripts-from-scm`.

With that we can keep our application code and the Jenkins pipeline definition conveniently together under revision control.

After we save the pipeline job, Jenkins will start polling the Git repository and trigger an execution whenever a change is detected (or you can click on **Build Now** to force a run).

Each successful build will result in an RPM package uploaded to our YUM repository. Go ahead and experiment, breaking the build by changing the `demo-app` source code so that the test fails.

To troubleshoot, look at the **Build History** list, select the job that failed and examine its **Console Output**:

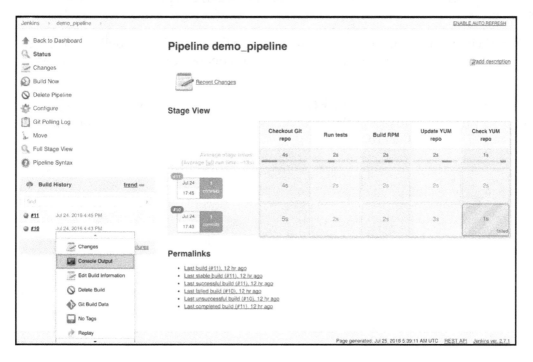

Now that you are familiar with our example pipeline, I encourage you to expand it: Add more stages to it, make some of the tasks execute in parallel, enable chat or email notifications, or link pipelines so they trigger each other.

You will appreciate the benefits of implementing a CI server as you continue to convert more of your daily, manual routines to Jenkins jobs.

You can be sure your teammates will love it too.

 Please remember to delete any AWS resources used in the preceding examples (VPC, EC2, S3, IAM, CodeCommit, etcetera) to avoid unnecessary charges.

Summary

In this chapter we studied examples of how to launch and configure a Continuous Integration environment on AWS.

We used our previous Terraform and SaltStack knowledge to prepare the AWS infrastructure.

With the help of Jenkins CI we composed a pipeline that would take application source code, run tests against it, build an RPM package and deposit that into a remote YUM repository for later use.

Our next topic will be on Continuous Delivery, an extension to Continuous Integration which takes us a step closer to being ready to deploy our application to a production environment with confidence.

5

Ever-Ready to Deploy Using Continuous Delivery

Thanks to the Continuous Integration setup we examined in the previous chapter, we now have a way of continuously producing deployable artifacts from our source code.

Our next goal will be to upgrade the pipeline from a Continuous Integration to an **Integration** plus **Delivery** one. To illustrate, we are in the middle of a three stage workflow:

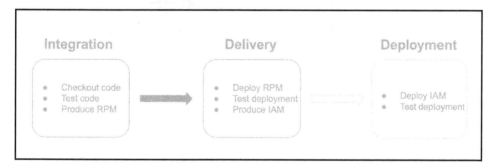

That is to say, following a successful Integration run, we trigger the Delivery stage that will do the following:

- Launch a vanilla EC2 instance
- Apply configuration management to it:
    - Install the `demo-app` RPM we produced
    - Install other required packages to turn it into a web server
- Test the applied configuration (using **Serverspec**)
- Produce an AMI out of the configured instance (using **Packer**)

- Launch an EC2 instance from the produced AMI
- Run additional tests against the new EC2 instance

This pipeline will ensure that the application RPM installs correctly, our configuration management gets applied as expected, and our new AMI artifact is fit for purpose. At the end we should be left with a sparkling, prebaked, production-ready AMI of a web server with our `demo-app` on it.

To accomplish these tasks, we are going to introduce two new tools to the mix – Packer and Serverspec (more details as we go).

We will be able to reuse a significant part of our work so far, given that we are building on top of it. As before, we will start by preparing our code, deploying it to AWS, and configuring our Jenkins Pipeline.

Feel free to skip some of the following steps if you have kept the AWS environment from the previous chapter running. Although I think that it might be better to start from scratch to avoid any confusion.

Preparing Terraform templates

In addition to the usual VPC, IGW, and subnet that we need for Jenkins, we are going to deploy NAT and ELB for our `demo-app` web server scenario.

Resources

Please refer to `https://github.com/PacktPublishing/Implementing-De vOps-on-AWS/blob/master/5585_05_CodeFiles/Terraform/resources. tf`.

We start with VPC, IGW, and NAT:

```
resource "aws_vpc" "terraform-vpc" {
  cidr_block = "${var.vpc-cidr}"
...

resource "aws_internet_gateway" "terraform-igw" {
  vpc_id = "${aws_vpc.terraform-vpc.id}"
}
```

```
resource "aws_eip" "nat-eip" {
  vpc = true
}

resource "aws_nat_gateway" "terraform-nat" {
  allocation_id = "${aws_eip.nat-eip.id}"
  subnet_id = "${aws_subnet.public-1.id}"
  depends_on = ["aws_internet_gateway.terraform-igw"]
...
```

We add a `public` subnet for Jenkins and ELB, plus a `private` one to be used by the EC2 web server:

```
resource "aws_route_table" "public" {
  vpc_id = "${aws_vpc.terraform-vpc.id}"
...
resource "aws_route_table" "private" {
  vpc_id = "${aws_vpc.terraform-vpc.id}"
...
```

Next is IAM. We need a role for Jenkins:

```
resource "aws_iam_role" "jenkins" {
    name = "jenkins"
    path = "/"
    assume_role_policy = <<EOF
{
```

And another one for the `demo-app` web server:

```
resource "aws_iam_role" "demo-app" {
    name = "demo-app"
    path = "/"
    assume_role_policy = <<EOF
{
```

They will be sharing a common policy, allowing them to access CodeCommit, where we keep our infrastructure and application code and S3, where we store our RPM artifacts:

```
resource "aws_iam_policy" "common" {
    name = "common"
    path = "/"
    policy = <<EOF
{
    "Version": "2012-10-17",
    "Statement": [
        {
            "Effect": "Allow",
```

```
    "Action": [
        "codecommit:Get*",
        "codecommit:GitPull",
        "codecommit:List*"
    ],
    "Resource": "*"
},
{
    "Effect": "Allow",
    "NotAction": [
        "s3:DeleteBucket"
    ],
    "Resource": "*"
...
```

The newcomer, Packer, is going to require a separate policy to allow for the manipulation of EC2 resources. We are going to use it to start/stop/terminate instances and create AMIs:

```
resource "aws_iam_policy" "jenkins" {
    name = "jenkins"
    path = "/"
    policy = <<EOF
{
    "Version": "2012-10-17",
    "Statement": [
        {
            "Effect": "Allow",
            "Action": [
                "ec2:AttachVolume",
                "ec2:CreateVolume",
                "ec2:DeleteVolume",
                "ec2:CreateKeypair",
                "ec2:DeleteKeypair",
                "ec2:DescribeSubnets"
...
            "Resource": "*",
        },
        {
            "Effect": "Allow",
            "Action": "iam:PassRole",
            "Resource": ["${aws_iam_role.demo-app.arn}"]
...
```

The need to allow `PassRole` represents an IAM security feature which helps prevent users/services granting themselves more privileges than they are supposed to have (refer to: `https://blogs.aws.amazon.com/security/post/Tx3M0IFB5XBOCQX/Granting-Permissi on-to-Launch-EC2-Instances-with-IAM-Roles-PassRole-Permission`).

We are going to need a security group for ELB, accepting HTTP traffic from the World:

```
resource "aws_security_group" "demo-app-elb" {
  name = "demo-app-elb"
  description = "ELB security group"
  vpc_id = "${aws_vpc.terraform-vpc.id}"

  ingress {
    from_port = "80"
    to_port = "80"
    protocol = "tcp"
    cidr_blocks = ["0.0.0.0/0"]
...
```

Then, ELB itself:

```
resource "aws_elb" "demo-app-elb" {
  name = "demo-app-elb"
  security_groups = ["${aws_security_group.demo-app-elb.id}"]
  subnets = ["${aws_subnet.public-1.id}"]

  listener {
    instance_port = 80
    instance_protocol = "http"
    lb_port = 80
    lb_protocol = "http"
...
```

We create a security group for Jenkins permitting SSH and HTTP/S traffic from anywhere:

```
resource "aws_security_group" "jenkins" {
  name = "jenkins"
  description = "ec2 instance security group"
  vpc_id = "${aws_vpc.terraform-vpc.id}"

ingress {
    from_port = "80"
    to_port = "80"
    protocol = "tcp"
    cidr_blocks = ["0.0.0.0/0"]
  }

  ingress {
```

```
        from_port = "443"
        to_port = "443"
        protocol = "tcp"
        cidr_blocks = ["0.0.0.0/0"]
  ...
```

The next one is for the web server, accepting HTTP from ELB and SSH from Jenkins:

```
resource "aws_security_group" "demo-app" {
  name = "demo-app"
  description = "ec2 instance security group"
  vpc_id = "${aws_vpc.terraform-vpc.id}"

  ingress {
    from_port = "80"
    to_port = "80"
    protocol = "tcp"
    security_groups = ["${aws_security_group.demo-app-elb.id}"]
  }

  ingress {
    from_port = "22"
    to_port = "22"
    protocol = "tcp"
    security_groups = ["${aws_security_group.jenkins.id}"]
  ...
```

To bootstrap the Jenkins node, we need the user-data we used in the past, with one important addition:

```
resource "aws_instance" "jenkins" {
  ...
    user_data = <<EOF
  ...
# Install SaltStack
yum -y install
https://repo.saltstack.com/yum/amazon/salt-amzn-repo-latest-1.ami.noarch.rp
m
yum clean expire-cache; yum -y install salt-minion; chkconfig salt-minion
off
# Put custom minion config in place (for enabling masterless mode)
cp -r /srv/salt/minion.d /etc/salt/
echo -e 'grains:\n roles:\n  - jenkins' > /etc/salt/minion.d/grains.conf
  ...
```

You will note that after we have installed SaltStack and put the masterless minion configuration in place, we also add a custom Grains file. The roles list that it holds will help us assign the Salt States later on (since we are now going to have two different types of hosts under configuration management: `jenkins` and our `demo-app` web server).

Variables

 Please refer to `https://github.com/PacktPublishing/Implementing-De vOps-on-AWS/blob/master/5585_05_CodeFiles/Terraform/variables. tf`.

No change from `Chapter 4`, *Build, Test, and Release Faster with Continuous Integration*, we set just a few VPC- and EC2 (Jenkins)-related variables.

Variables (values)

 Please refer to `https://github.com/PacktPublishing/Implementing-De vOps-on-AWS/blob/master/5585_05_CodeFiles/Terraform/terraform. tfvars`.

Same as our previous deployment, we specify the values for the VPC and Jenkins variables.

Outputs

 Please refer to `https://github.com/PacktPublishing/Implementing-De vOps-on-AWS/blob/master/5585_05_CodeFiles/Terraform/outputs.tf`.

Some new `outputs` reflect the additional `resources`. The ELB endpoint and the ID of our Private subnet and the `demo-app` security group:

```
output "ELB URI" {
  value = "${aws_elb.demo-app-elb.dns_name}"
}
output "Private subnet ID" {
  value = "${aws_subnet.private-1.id}"
```

```
}
output "Demo-app secgroup" {
  value = "${aws_security_group.demo-app.id}"
}
```

This is certainly not an exhaustive list, and if we need more information later, we can always retrieve a detailed description of our deployed infrastructure via the `terraform show` command.

Prepareing Salt code

We will be using SaltStack to apply configuration management on both our Jenkins and `demo-app` web server nodes. We will be using Grains to define which States/Pillars apply to which host. Let us have a look at the code:

States

Please refer to `https://github.com/PacktPublishing/Implementing-De vOps-on-AWS/tree/master/5585_05_CodeFiles/CodeCommit/salt/stat es`.

top.sls

The `top` file shows us that some states are shared between all hosts/roles while others are assigned based on the role:

```
base:
  '*':
    - users
    - yum-s3

  'roles:jenkins':
    - match: grain
    - jenkins
    - nginx.jenkins
    - docker
    - packer

  'roles:demo-app':
    - match: grain
```

```
      - php-fpm
      - nginx.demo-app
      - demo-app
```

You are already familiar with the users and the yum-s3 States. Now this is a good time to add an account and an SSH key for yourself.

jenkins

We install the service as before plus a couple of extra tools:

```
jenkins_prereq:
  pkg.installed:
    - pkgs:
...
        - jq
      - httpd-tools
...
```

We will be using jq to parse JSON output and ab from the httpd-tools package for basic HTTP load testing.

nginx

This time we split the NGINX State into three parts:

init.sls

This installs the main package and sets up the service daemon:

```
nginx:
  pkg.installed: []

  service.running:
    - enable: True
    - reload: True
    - require:
      - pkg: nginx
```

jenkins.sls

This deploys the NGINX configuration and related file needed for the Jenkins service:

```
include:
  - nginx

/etc/nginx/conf.d/jenkins.conf:
  file.managed:
    - source: salt://nginx/files/jenkins.conf
...
```

demo-app.sls

This deploys the NGINX configuration and related file needed for the `demo-app` web server:

```
include:
  - nginx

/etc/nginx/conf.d/demo-app.conf:
  file.managed:
    - source: salt://nginx/files/demo-app.conf
```

In both cases, we include `init.sls` also known as NGINX, which provides shared functionality, Docker remains the same, whereas Packer is a new addition which we will get to play with shortly:

```
packer:
  archive.extracted:
    - name: /opt/
    - source:
'https://releases.hashicorp.com/packer/0.10.1/packer_0.10.1_linux_amd64.zip
'
    - source_hash: md5=3a54499fdf753e7e7c682f5d704f684f
    - archive_format: zip
    - if_missing: /opt/packer

  cmd.wait:
    - name: 'chmod +x /opt/packer'
    - watch:
      - archive: packer
```

The archive module conveniently downloads and extracts the Packer zip file for us. After that we ensure that the binary is executable with `cmd.wait`, which gets triggered on package change (that is watch archive).

php-fpm

We need PHP in order to be able to serve our PHP `application (demo-app)`:

```
include:
  - nginx

php-fpm:
  pkg.installed:
    - name: php-fpm
    - require:
      - pkg: nginx

  service.running:
    - name: php-fpm
    - enable: True
    - reload: True
    - require_in:
      - service: nginx
...
```

And finally, the `demo-app` State, which installs a selected version the application `rpm`. We will discuss how we populate `/tmp/APP_VERSION` a bit later:

```
{% set APP_VERSION = salt['cmd.run']('cat /tmp/APP_VERSION') %}

include:
  - nginx

demo-app:
  pkg.installed:
    - name: demo-app
    - version: {{ APP_VERSION }}
    - require_in:
      - service: nginx
```

Pillars

 Please refer to
https://github.com/PacktPublishing/Implementing-DevOps-on-AWS/tr
ee/master/5585_05_CodeFiles/CodeCommit/salt/pillars.

We will reuse the `nginx` and `users` Pillars from the previous chapter.

Minion configuration

 Please refer to `https://github.com/PacktPublishing/Implementing-De`
`vOps-on-AWS/tree/master/5585_05_CodeFiles/CodeCommit/salt/mini`
`on.d`.

While `masterless.conf` remains the same as before, we are extending the `minion` configuration with a custom role Grain, which we set via UserData for Jenkins and a config file for the `demo-app` web server (discussed later in the chapter).

Preparing Jenkins code

Before we proceed with Jenkins, allow me to introduce the two new helpers – Packer and Serverspec.

Packer

 Please refer to `https://github.com/PacktPublishing/Implementing-De`
`vOps-on-AWS/tree/master/5585_05_CodeFiles/CodeCommit/demo-app-`
`cdelivery/packer`.

As described:

> *"Packer is a tool for creating machine and container images for multiple platforms from a single source configuration."*
>
> *– https://www.packer.io*

Essentially, Packer is going to, well, pack things for us. We will feed it a template, based on which it will launch an EC2 instance, perform requested tasks (over SSH), then create an AMI from it. Packer can talk to various platforms (AWS, GCE, OpenStack, and so on) to provision resources via local shell, remote (SSH), Salt, Ansible, Chef, and others. As a HashiCorp product, it does not come as a surprise that Packer uses a templating system very similar to Terraform's.

demo-app.json

Here, we define what and how it should be provisioned. At the top, we set our `variables`:

```json
"variables": {
  "srcAmiId": null,
  "amiName": null,
  "sshUser": null,
  "instanceProfile": null,
  "subnetId": null,
  "vpcId": null,
  "userDataFile": null,
  "appVersion": null
}
...
```

We have exported the actual values to a `variables` file (see later). Setting a value to null here, makes it required. We could also fix values here or make use of environment variables (refer to `https://www.packer.io/docs/templates/user-variables.html`). Once defined, you can refer to variables with this syntax: `{{user `srcAmiId`}}`.

The next section lists the `builders`, in our case, AWS EC2:

```json
"builders": [{
  "type": "amazon-ebs",
  "region": "us-east-1",
  "source_ami": "{{user `srcAmiId`}}",
  "instance_type": "t2.nano",
  "ssh_username": "{{user `sshUser`}}",
  "ami_name": "{{user `amiName`}}-{{timestamp}}",
  "iam_instance_profile": "{{user `instanceProfile`}}",
  "subnet_id": "{{user `subnetId`}}",
  "vpc_id": "{{user `vpcId`}}",
  "user_data_file": "{{user `userDataFile`}}",
  "run_tags": {
    "Name": "Packer ({{user `amiName`}}-{{timestamp}})",
    "CreatedBy": "Jenkins"
  },
  "tags": {
    "Name": "{{user `amiName`}}-{{timestamp}}",
    "CreatedBy": "Jenkins"
  }
}]
```

We are asking for an EBS-backed nano instance in the US-East-1 region. It is to be bootstrapped via UserData (see later in the text) and tagged as `"CreatedBy": "Jenkins"`.

Naturally, after launching the instance, we would like to provision it:

```
"provisioners": [
    {
        "type": "shell",
        "inline": [
          "echo 'Waiting for the instance to fully boot up...'",
          "sleep 30" ,
          "echo "Setting APP_VERSION to {{user `appVersion`}}"",
          "echo "{{user `appVersion`}}" > /tmp/APP_VERSION"
          ]
    }
```

Here, our first `provisioners` is a shell command to be executed over SSH by Packer (refer to `https://www.packer.io/docs/provisioners/shell.html`). It pauses for 30 seconds to allow the node to complete its boot process, then creates the `APP_VERSION` file needed by the Salt `php-fpm` State.

Next, we run SaltStack:

```
{
        "type": "salt-masterless",
        "skip_bootstrap": true,
        "local_state_tree": "salt/states",
        "local_pillar_roots": "salt/pillars"
}
```

Packer already knows how to run Salt via the salt-masterless `provisioner`. It only needs a source of States and Pillars (refer to:
`https://www.packer.io/docs/provisioners/salt-masterless.html`). We define a relative path of `salt/`, which is part of a checked out Git repository (see `demo-app-cdelivery` here). We are opting to install Salt via UserData, hence `skip_bootstrap: true`.

We will get to Serverspec in a moment, but here is how we run it:

```
{
        "type": "file",
        "source": "serverspec",
        "destination": "/tmp/"
},
{
        "type": "shell",
        "inline": [
          "echo 'Installing Serverspec tests...'",
          "sudo gem install --no-document rake serverspec",
          "echo 'Running Serverspec tests...'",
          "cd /tmp/serverspec && sudo /usr/local/bin/rake spec"
```

```
      ]
   }
```

The file `provisioners` is used to transfer data between the remote instance and Packer (refer to `https://www.packer.io/docs/provisioners/file.html`). We push the local `"serverspec/"` folder containing our Serverspec tests to `"/tmp"` on the remote side. Then, run a few shell commands to install the Serverspec ruby gem and run the tests.

demo-app_vars.json

The values for the variables we defined earlier (alternatively, you could set these as a list of `-var 'key=value'` cmd line arguments):

```
{
    "srcAmiId": "ami-6869aa05",
    "amiName": "demo-app",
    "sshUser": "ec2-user",
    "instanceProfile": "demo-app",
    "subnetId": "subnet-4d1c2467",
    "vpcId": "vpc-bd6f0bda",
    "userDataFile": "packer/demo-app_userdata.sh"
}
```

demo-app_userdata.sh

The EC2 UserData to bootstrap our test instance:

```
#!/bin/bash

set -euf -o pipefail
exec 1> >(logger -s -t $(basename $0)) 2>&1

# Install SaltStack
yum -y install
https://repo.saltstack.com/yum/amazon/salt-amzn-repo-latest-1.ami.noarch.rp
m
yum clean expire-cache; yum -y install salt-minion; chkconfig salt-minion
off

# Put custom grains in place
echo -e 'grains:\n roles:\n  - demo-app' > /etc/salt/minion.d/grains.conf
```

Much like the one we use for Jenkins. It gets SaltStack installed and puts the roles Grain in place.

Serverspec

 Please refer to `https://github.com/PacktPublishing/Implementing-De vOps-on-AWS/tree/master/5585_05_CodeFiles/CodeCommit/demo-app-cdelivery/serverspec`.

Straight out of the front page:

> *"RSpec tests for your servers configured by CFEngine, Puppet, Ansible, Itamae or anything else.*
> *With Serverspec, you can write RSpec tests for checking your servers are configured correctly.*
> *Serverspec tests your servers' actual state by executing command locally, via SSH, via WinRM, via Docker API and so on. So you don't need to install any agent softwares on your servers and can use any configuration management tools, Puppet, Ansible, CFEngine, Itamae and so on.*
> *But the true aim of Serverspec is to help refactoring infrastructure code."*
> *– http://serverspec.org*

We are going to use Serverspec to assert the final state of the EC2 instance after all other configuration tasks have been completed. It should help verify that any nonconfiguration management changes have taken effect (for example, shell commands) and that configuration management has been applied correctly (for example, no race conditions/overlaps/conflicts in States). This does introduce some overhead and some will rightly question whether it is needed in addition to a SaltStack run, so it remains a personal preference. I see it as a second layer of verification or a safety net.

The content under the `serverspec/` folder has been created by running `serverspec-init` (refer to `http://serverspec.org`), selecting UNIX and then SSH. We replace the sample `spec.rb` file with our own:

spec/localhost/demo-app_spec.rb

```
require 'spec_helper'

versionFile = open('/tmp/APP_VERSION')
appVersion = versionFile.read.chomp

describe package("demo-app-#{appVersion}") do
  it { should be_installed }
end
```

```
describe service('php-fpm') do
  it { should be_enabled }
  it { should be_running }
end

describe service('nginx') do
  it { should be_enabled }
  it { should be_running }
end

describe user('veselin') do
  it { should exist }
  it { should have_authorized_key 'ssh-rsa ...' }
end
```

Serverspec performs tests on supported resource types (refer to `http://serverspec.org/resource_types.html`).

In the preceding brief example we assert that:

- A specific version of our `demo-app` package has been installed
- PHP-FPM and NGINX are running and enabled on boot
- The SSH `authorized_keys` file for a given user has the expected contents

Our Serverspec tests can be run from the containing folder like so:

cd /tmp/serverspec && sudo /usr/local/bin/rake spec

It will parse any files it finds ending in `_spec.rb`. We use `sudo` only because, in this case, we are trying to read a private file (`authorized_keys`).

And back to Jenkins. We are already familiar with the concept of a `Jenkinsfile` (as used by our Integration job). In this example, we will be adding a second (Delivery) pipeline using the same approach.

Let us examine both pipeline jobs.

demo-app

 Please refer to `https://github.com/PacktPublishing/Implementing-De vOps-on-AWS/blob/master/5585_05_CodeFiles/CodeCommit/demo-app /Jenkinsfile`.

This is our old Integration job that downloads the application code, runs tests against it, produces an RPM package and uploads the package to a YUM repository. We are going to add one more stage to this process:

```
stage "Trigger downstream"
    build job: "demo-app-cdelivery",
    parameters: [[$class: "StringParameterValue", name: "APP_VERSION",
value:
    "${gitHash}-1"]], wait: false
```

This final stage triggers our next job that is the Delivery pipeline and passes an APP_VERSION parameter to it.

The value of this parameter is the gitHash which we have been using so far as a version string for our demo-app RPM package.

The -1 you see appended to the gitHash represents the rpm's minor version number which you can safely ignore at this time.

Setting wait to false means that we don't want to keep the current job running, waiting for the subsequently triggered one to complete.

demo-app-cdelivery

 Please refer to https://github.com/PacktPublishing/Implementing-De vOps-on-AWS/blob/master/5585_05_CodeFiles/CodeCommit/demo-app-cdelivery/Jenkinsfile.

Now the fun part. The Delivery job has been passed an APP_VERSION and is ready to start, let us follow the process described in the Jenkinsfile.

We start by cleaning up our workspace, checking out the demo-app-cdelivery repository, then adding the SaltStack code on top of it. We need both codebases in order to launch an instance and configure it to be a web server:

```
#!groovy

node {

    step([$class: 'WsCleanup'])

    stage "Checkout Git repo"
```

```
    checkout scm

  stage "Checkout additional repos"
    dir("salt") {
      git "https://git-codecommit.us-east-1.amazonaws.com/v1/repos/salt"
    }
```

After this, we are ready to run Packer:

```
  stage "Run Packer"
      sh "/opt/packer validate -var="appVersion=$APP_VERSION" -var-
  file=packer/demo-app_vars.json packer/demo-app.json"
      sh "/opt/packer build -machine-readable -var="appVersion=$APP_VERSION"
  -var-file=packer/demo-app_vars.json packer/demo-app.json | tee
  packer/packer.log"
```

First, we validate our template and then execute, requesting a machine-readable output.
Packer is going to spin up an instance, connect over SSH to it, apply all relevant Salt States,
run Serverspec tests, and produce an AMI of what is essentially a web server that has the
demo-app and all its prerequisites installed.

Then, we go ahead and launch a second EC2 instance; this time, form the AMI we just
created:

```
  stage "Deploy AMI"
      def amiId = sh returnStdout: true, script:"tail -n1 packer/packer.log |
  awk '{printf \$NF}'"
      def ec2Keypair = "terraform"
      def secGroup = "sg-2708ef5d"
      def instanceType = "t2.nano"
      def subnetId = "subnet-4d1c2467"
      def instanceProfile = "demo-app"
      echo "Launching an instance from ${amiId}"
      sh "aws ec2 run-instances \
          --region us-east-1 \
          --image-id ${amiId} \
          --key-name ${ec2Keypair} \
          --security-group-ids ${secGroup} \
          --instance-type ${instanceType} \
          --subnet-id ${subnetId} \
          --iam-instance-profile Name=${instanceProfile} \
          | tee .ec2_run-instances.log \
          "
      def instanceId = sh returnStdout: true, script: "printf \$(jq
  .Instances[0].InstanceId < .ec2_run-instances.log)"
```

The variables seen at the top we get from Terraform (terraform show).

We use the `aws cli` to launch the instance inside the Private VPC subnet, attach the demo-app security group, the Terraform key, and `demo-app` instance profile to it. You will notice that we need not pass any EC2 credentials here as Jenkins is already authorized via the IAM role we assigned to it earlier.

Next, we retrieve the `instanceId` by parsing the `aws cli` JSON output with `jq` (refer to `https://stedolan.github.io/jq`).

After we have launched the instance, we set its tags, register it with ELB, and loop until its ELB status becomes `InService`:

```
sh "aws ec2 create-tags --resources ${instanceId} \
        --region us-east-1 \
        --tags Key=Name,Value="Jenkins (demo-app-$APP_VERSION)"
        Key=CreatedBy,Value=Jenkins \ \
        "

    echo "Registering with ELB"
    def elbId = "demo-app-elb"
    sh "aws elb register-instances-with-load-balancer \
        --region us-east-1 \
        --load-balancer-name ${elbId} \
        --instances ${instanceId} \
        "

    echo "Waiting for the instance to come into service"
    sh "while [ "x\$(aws elb describe-instance-health --region us-east-1 --
load-
    balancer-name ${elbId} --instances ${instanceId} |
    jq .InstanceStates[].State | tr -d '"')" != "xInService" ]; do : ;
sleep 60;
    done"
```

Now that the node is ready to serve, we can launch our improvised Load Test using AB:

```
    stage "Run AB test"
    def elbUri =
"http://demo-app-elb-1931064195.us-east-1.elb.amazonaws.com/"
    sh "ab -c5 -n1000 -d -S ${elbUri} | tee .ab.log"
    def non2xx = sh returnStdout: true, script:"set -o pipefail;(grep
'Non-2xx' .ab.log | awk '{printf \$NF}') || (printf 0)"
    def writeErr = sh returnStdout: true, script:"grep 'Write errors'
.ab.log | awk '{printf \$NF}'"
    def failedReqs = sh returnStdout: true, script:"grep 'Failed requests'
.ab.log | awk '{printf \$NF}'"
    def rps = sh returnStdout: true, script:"grep 'Requests per second'
.ab.log | awk '{printf \$4}' | awk -F. '{printf \$1}'"
```

```
    def docLen = sh returnStdout: true, script:"grep 'Document Length'
.ab.log | awk '{printf \$3}'"

    echo "Non2xx=${non2xx}, WriteErrors=${writeErr},
FailedReqs=${failedReqs}, ReqsPerSec=${rps}, DocLength=${docLen}"
    sh "if [ ${non2xx} -gt 10 ] || [ ${writeErr} -gt 10 ] || [
${failedReqs} -gt 10 ] || [ ${rps} -lt 1000 ] || [ ${docLen} -lt 10 ]; then
\
        echo "ERR: AB test failed" | tee -a .error.log; \
    fi \
    "
```

At the end of the AB test, the various reported metrics are compared with preset thresholds and logged.

The EC2 instance is no longer needed, so it can be terminated:

```
stage "Terminate test instance"
    sh "aws ec2 terminate-instances --region us-east-1 --instance-ids
${instanceId}"
```

In the final stage, the job's exit code is determined by the AB test results:

```
stage "Verify test results"
    sh "if [ -s '.error.log' ]; then \
        cat '.error.log'; \
        :> '.error.log'; \
        exit 100; \
    else \
        echo 'Tests OK'; \
    fi \
    "
```

Preparing CodeCommit repositories

Ideally, we would put all the preceding code under revision control, so let us create some repositories. We need an IAM user with enough privileges to do that:

 Please refer to `https://github.com/PacktPublishing/Implementing-De vOps-on-AWS/blob/master/5585_05_CodeFiles/CodeCommit/demo-app-cdelivery/Jenkinsfile`.

```
{
    "Version": "2012-10-17",
    "Statement": [
```

```
{
        "Effect": "Allow",
        "NotAction": [
            "codecommit:DeleteRepository"
        ],
        "Resource": "*"
},
{
        "Effect": "Allow",
        "NotAction": [
            "s3:DeleteBucket"
        ],
        "Resource": "*"
},
{
        "Sid": "Stmt1461764665000",
        "Effect": "Allow",
        "Action": [
            "ec2:AllocateAddress",
            "ec2:AssociateAddress",
    ...
```

We create a `terraform` IAM user with the preceding policy that grants us privileges to carry out the CodeCommit tasks and also do the Terraform deployment later (remember to write down the API keys).

Please refer to the previous chapter on how to export the API keys and create three CodeCommit repositories: `salt`, `demo-app`, and `demo-app-cdelivery`.

You will need to clone the repositories locally and populate each with the code we prepared earlier respectively (refer to: `https://github.com/PacktPublishing/Implementing-DevOps-on-AWS/tree/master/5585_05_CodeFiles/CodeCommit`).

Deploy Terraform templates

Create a `terraform` EC2 key pair, then run terraform plan, terraform validate, and finally terraform apply inside the Terraform templates folder (if needed, please refer to the previous chapter for details on how to do all of this).

Initializing Jenkins

Once Terraform has finished the deployment, you will get the Jenkins EIP value in the outputs. Do a hostname lookup on it and load the resulting address in your browser. You should see the **Getting Started** page (screenshots and instructions in previous chapter):

- Unlock jenkins
- Install suggested plugins
- Create an Admin user

Configuring Jenkins jobs

Prior to recreating the Continuous Integration pipeline job, we need a S3 bucket for our YUM repository. Create a bucket (unless you've kept the old one around), update the `demo-app/Jenkinsfile` script accordingly then commit and push Git changes upstream.

demo-app pipeline

Refer to the *Setting up the pipeline* steps from the previous chapter to create the Continuous Integration job. Let us call it `demo-app` this time around. The script path remains the same (`https://git-codecommit.us-east-1.amazonaws.com/v1/repos/demo-app`).

You should now have this:

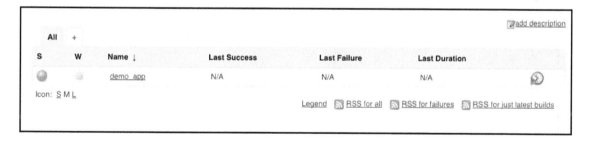

The pipeline is going to fail as we do not have our YUM repository configured yet:

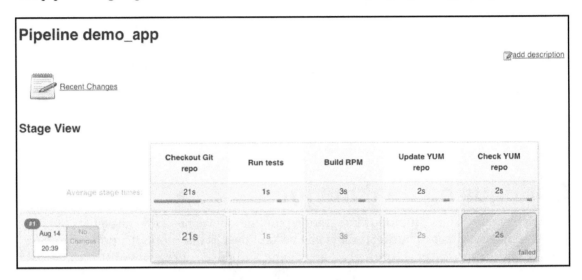

The repository contents have already been uploaded to S3 by this first job run. Now we need to update the salt/states/yum-s3/files/s3.repo file with the S3 URL and set the repository to enabled. Commit and push the Salt changes to the Git repository, then pull and apply on the Jenkins node.

A subsequent pipeline run takes us a step further:

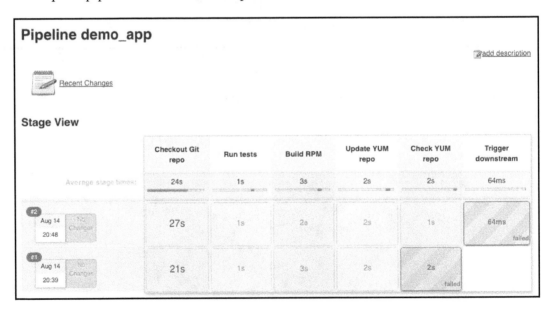

This time the failure is because our downstream job is not quite ready yet. Let us fix that next.

demo-app-cdelivery pipeline

From the Jenkin's dashboard, we select **New Item**:

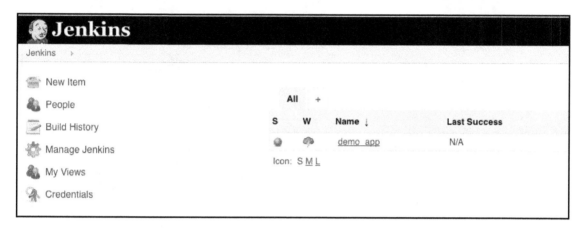

We shall call it `demo-app-cdelivery`:

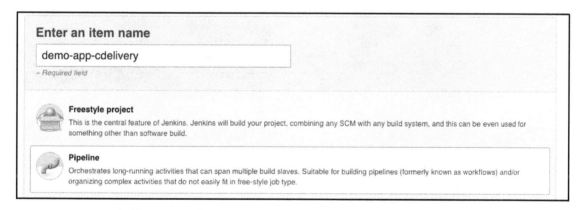

This job will be triggered by another one, so no need to poll SCM. Also, we have a parameter being passed to this pipeline:

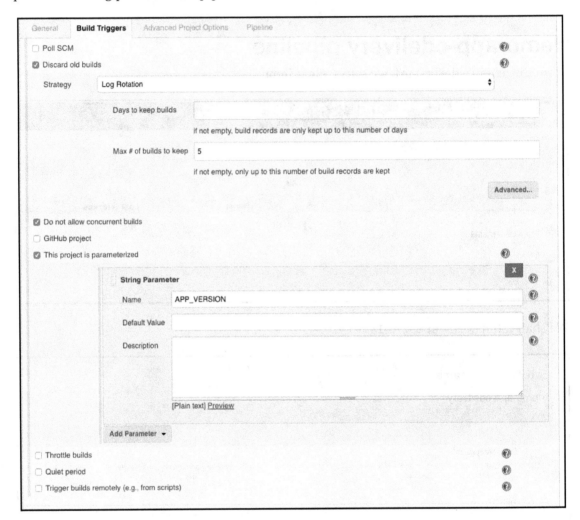

Finally, we set the location of the Jenkinsfile
(https://git-codecommit.us-east-1.amazonaws.com/v1/repos/demo-app-cdelivery):

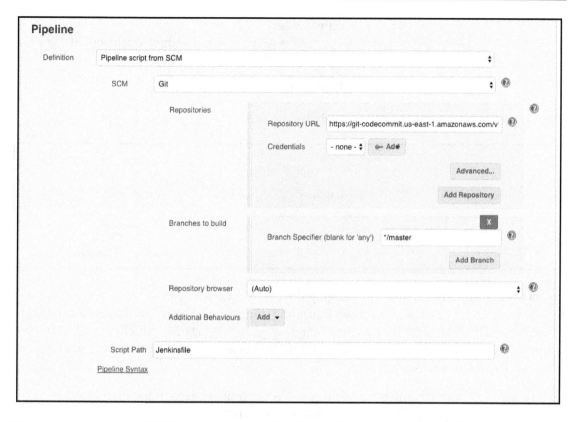

Do you remember the VPC details we specified in the Packer `variables` file and also the `Jenkinsfile` for this pipeline? We need to set those to match our current VPC:

- Update the variables in `packer/demo-app_vars.json`
  - `srcAmiId` could be the latest AmazonLinux AMI
  - `subnetId` is the ID of the Private subnet
  - `vpcId`
- Update `demo-app-cdelivery/Jenkinsfile`:
  - In the **Deploy AMI** stage:
    - `secGroup` is the ID of the `demo-app` security group
    - `subnetId` is the ID of the Private VPC subnet as mentioned earlier

- In **Run AB test**
  - `elbUri` is the endpoint address of the `demo-app-elb` ELB

- Commit and push your changes.

Here, we are with our two pipelines ready for action:

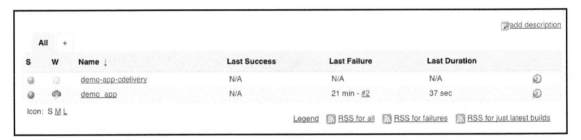

Let us trigger a `demo-app` run by changing the `$full_name` in `demo-app/src/index.php`. You should see it running after detecting the Git change. At the end of the run, it should trigger the downstream `demo-app-cdelivery` pipeline, and after another approximately10 minutes, there should be a brand new `demo-app` AMI waiting for you (check the AWS console).

Please remember to delete any AWS resources used in the mentioned examples (VPC, EC2, S3, IAM, CodeCommit, and so on) to avoid unnecessary charges.

Summary

In this chapter, we extended our Jenkins pipeline to deploy and test our application artifact on an EC2 instance in a VPC environment. You learned how to use Packer to template the provisioning of instances as well as how to use Serverspec to apply extra verification of our infrastructure.

In the next chapter, we are going to finalize our Jenkins pipeline setup by adding the Continuous Deployment element to it. We will examine ways to deploy AMIs created during the Delivery stage into a production environment.

6

Continuous Deployment - A Fully Automated Workflow

Welcome to the final stage of the CI workflow – the **Continuous Deployment**.

We are now ready to take the AMI we produced during the Continuous Delivery step and deploy that to production.

For this process, we are going to use **blue/green deployment** approach. Our production environment is going to consist of ELB and two Auto scaling Groups (blue and green):

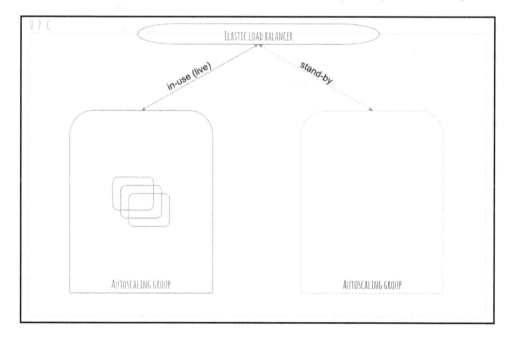

If we assume that the blue group holds our current production nodes, then upon deployment, we do the following:

1. Attach ELB to the green group
2. Scale the green group up using the new AMI
3. Check for errors
4. Scale the blue group down, effectively shifting traffic to the instances of the new AMI

As we are building on top of our existing CI pipelines, there are only a few changes we need to make to the code from the previous chapter. We need to add a few extra Terraform resources; let us take a look at those.

Terraform code (resources.tf)

 Please refer to: `https://github.com/PacktPublishing/Implementing-D evOps-on-AWS/blob/master/5585_06_CodeFiles/Terraform/resources .tf`.

We add a second public and a matching private subnet so that we can distribute the production instances across multiple availability zones.

The `aws_subnet` resource creates a subnet named `public-2`. It takes attributes such as a VPC ID, CIDR BLOCK and AZs, the values of which we pull from variables. To compute the CIDR and AZ values we use Terraform's interpolation functions (ref: `https://www.terraform.io/docs/configuration/interpolation.html`):

```
resource "aws_subnet" "public-2" {
  vpc_id = "${aws_vpc.terraform-vpc.id}"
  cidr_block = "${cidrsubnet(var.vpc-cidr, 8, 3)}"
  availability_zone = "${element(split(",",var.aws-availability-zones),
count.index + 1)}"
  map_public_ip_on_launch = true

  tags {
    Name = "Public"
  }
}
```

Next, we associate the newly created subnet with a routing table:

```
resource "aws_route_table_association" "public-2" {
  subnet_id = "${aws_subnet.public-2.id}"
  route_table_id = "${aws_route_table.public.id}"
}
```

Then repeat for the `Private` subnet:

```
resource "aws_subnet" "private-2" {
  vpc_id = "${aws_vpc.terraform-vpc.id}"
  cidr_block = "${cidrsubnet(var.vpc-cidr, 8, 4)}"
  availability_zone = "${element(split(",",var.aws-availability-zones),
count.index +1)}"
  map_public_ip_on_launch = false

  tags {
    Name = "Private"
  }
}

resource "aws_route_table_association" "private-2" {
  subnet_id = "${aws_subnet.private-2.id}"
  route_table_id = "${aws_route_table.private.id}"
}
```

In this VPC, we are going to end up with subnets 1 and 3 public, and 2 and 4 private.

The next change is the addition of a prod ELB and a security group for it:

```
resource "aws_security_group" "demo-app-elb-prod" {
  name = "demo-app-elb-prod"
  description = "ELB security group"
  vpc_id = "${aws_vpc.terraform-vpc.id}"

  ingress {
    from_port = "80"
    to_port = "80"
    protocol = "tcp"
    cidr_blocks = ["0.0.0.0/0"]
  }
```

Note the protocol value of `"-1"`, meaning "all":

```
egress {
  from_port = 0
  to_port = 0
  protocol = "-1"
  cidr_blocks = ["0.0.0.0/0"]
}

}

resource "aws_elb" "demo-app-elb-prod" {
  name = "demo-app-elb-prod"
  security_groups = ["${aws_security_group.demo-app-elb-prod.id}"]
  subnets = ["${aws_subnet.public-1.id}", "${aws_subnet.public-2.id}"]
  cross_zone_load_balancing = true
  connection_draining = true
  connection_draining_timeout = 30

  listener {
    instance_port = 80
    instance_protocol = "http"
    lb_port = 80
    lb_protocol = "http"
  }

  tags {
    Name = "demo-app-elb-prod"
  }
}
```

Let us also update the `demo-app` security group Ingress rules to allow traffic from the ELB. To help visualize, here is our earlier diagram with more labels:

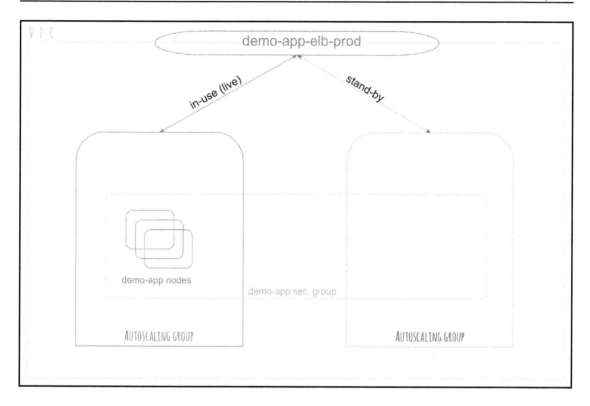

And in code:

```
resource "aws_security_group" "demo-app" {
  name = "demo-app"
  description = "ec2 instance security group"
  vpc_id = "${aws_vpc.terraform-vpc.id}"

  ingress {
    from_port = "80"
    to_port = "80"
    protocol = "tcp"
    security_groups = ["${aws_security_group.demo-app-elb.id}",
"${aws_security_group.demo-app-elb-prod.id}"]
  }
```

Then we introduce our blue/green **Auto Scaling Groups** (**ASG**) and a temporary launch configuration:

```
resource "aws_launch_configuration" "demo-app-lcfg" {
    name = "placeholder_launch_config"
    image_id = "${var.jenkins-ami-id}"
    instance_type = "${var.jenkins-instance-type}"
    iam_instance_profile = "${aws_iam_instance_profile.demo-app.id}"
    security_groups = ["${aws_security_group.demo-app.id}"]
}

resource "aws_autoscaling_group" "demo-app-blue" {
  name = "demo-app-blue"
  launch_configuration = "${aws_launch_configuration.demo-app-lcfg.id}"
  vpc_zone_identifier = ["${aws_subnet.private-1.id}",
"${aws_subnet.private-2.id}"]
  min_size = 0
  max_size = 0

  tag {
    key = "ASG"
    value = "demo-app-blue"
    propagate_at_launch = true
  }
}

resource "aws_autoscaling_group" "demo-app-green" {
  name = "demo-app-green"
  launch_configuration = "${aws_launch_configuration.demo-app-lcfg.id}"
  vpc_zone_identifier = ["${aws_subnet.private-1.id}",
"${aws_subnet.private-2.id}"]
  min_size = 0
  max_size = 0

  tag {
    key = "ASG"
    value = "demo-app-green"
    propagate_at_launch = true
  }
}
```

The launch configuration here is really only a placeholder, so that we can define the Auto Scaling Groups (which is why we reuse the Jenkins variables). We are going to create a new, real launch configuration to serve the demo-app later on as part of the pipeline.

outputs.tf

 Please refer to: `https://github.com/PacktPublishing/Implementing-D`
`evOps-on-AWS/blob/master/5585_06_CodeFiles/Terraform/outputs.t`
`f.`

A minor addition to the outputs, to give us the Production ELB endpoint:

```
output "ELB URI PROD" {
  value = "${aws_elb.demo-app-elb-prod.dns_name}"
}
```

Deployment

It is time for exercise. Using the earlier-mentioned templates and the rest of the familiar code from `https://github.com/PacktPublishing/Implementing-DevOps-on-AWS/tree` `/master/5585_06_CodeFiles` plus your previous experience you should be able to bring up a VPC plus a Jenkins instance with two pipelines, exactly as we did in the chapter on Continuous Delivery. Do not forget to update any deployment-specific details such as the following:

- The SSH public key in `salt:states:users:files`
- The authorized key in the `serverspec` test specification
- The S3 URI in `salt:states:yum-s3:files:s3.repo`
- The S3 bucket name in `demo-app/Jenkinsfile`
- The variables in `packer:demo-app_vars.json`
- The variables in `demo-app-cdelivery/Jenkinsfile`

I would recommend you to disable the SCM Polling in the **demo-app** job so that we don't trigger a run before all our downstream jobs have been configured.

Assuming that all went well, we are back where we left off:

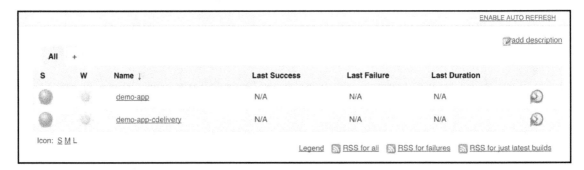

Jenkins pipelines

Earlier we have our Integration and Delivery pipelines chained together, taking code and producing and AMI artifact. Our next task is to design a third pipeline to take that AMI and deploy it into our production environment.

Before we can create the new job in Jenkins, we need to make the code for it available via Git:

 Please refer to: `https://github.com/PacktPublishing/Implementing-D evOps-on-AWS/tree/master/5585_06_CodeFiles/CodeCommit/demo-app -cdeployment.`

We will examine the files in detail shortly, for now just create and populate a `demo-app- cdeployment` CodeCommit repository. Similar to our other repositories, the new one would have an URL such as `https://git-codecommit.us-east-1.amazonaws.com/v1/repos/demo-app-cdeployment.`

With that in hand, we proceed to create the pipeline:

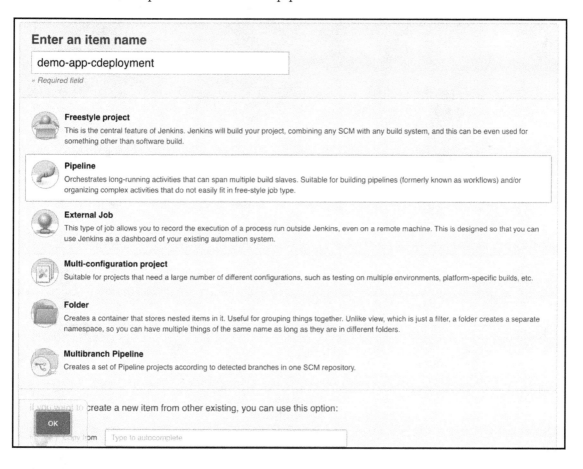

It will need to take an `AMI ID` parameter (to be passed on from the Delivery job):

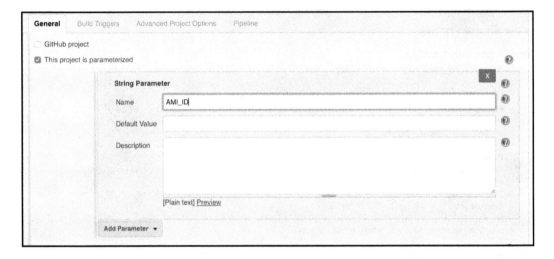

Then of course, it needs the `Jenkinsfile` location
(`https://git-codecommit.us-east-1.amazonaws.com/v1/repos/demo-app-cdeployment`):

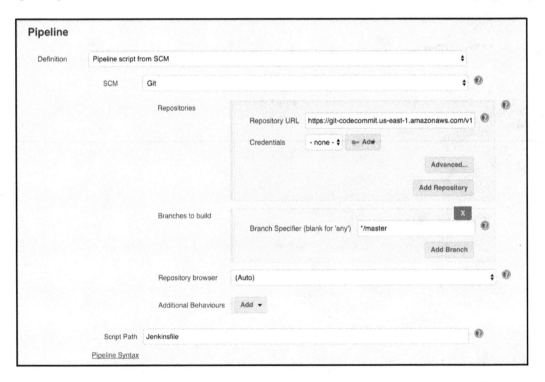

With that final job ready, our Jenkins dashboard looks like this:

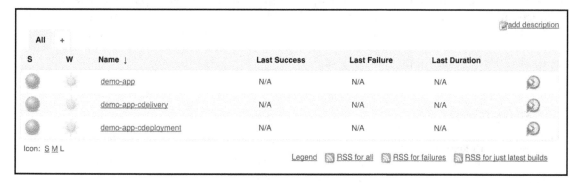

Continuous Deployment pipeline

Back to the code, as promised:

 Please refer to `https://github.com/PacktPublishing/Implementing-De
vOps-on-AWS/blob/master/5585_06_CodeFiles/CodeCommit/demo-app-
cdeployment/Jenkinsfile`.

Our Jenkinsfile is rather simple:

```groovy
#!groovy

node {
  step([$class: 'WsCleanup'])

  stage "Checkout Git repo" {
    checkout scm
  }

  stage "Deploy AMI" {
    sh returnStdout: false, script: "bash ./cdeployment.sh ${AMI_ID}"
  }

}
```

We simply check out the associated repository and execute a shell script. Naturally, we could have coded the whole task in Groovy, but I personally am more used to Bash, hence the resulting `cdeployment.sh`.

We briefly described the deployment task in the beginning of this chapter. Generally speaking, we are going to be serving the application code from two separate clusters of instances and swap traffic from one to the other. We will use the extensive and user friendly AWS CLI to carry out most operations plus Bash to process any input/output data.

Let us dive into the script for more details.

cdeployment.sh

Please refer to
https://github.com/PacktPublishing/Implementing-DevOps-on-AWS/bl
ob/master/5585_06_CodeFiles/CodeCommit/demo-app-
cdeployment/cdeployment.sh.

At the top, we define the names of our Auto Scaling Groups, the Production ELB, and the ID of the AMI, which we will be working with (passed on from the upstream pipeline):

```
#!/bin/bash
set -ef -o pipefail

blueGroup="demo-app-blue"
greenGroup="demo-app-green"
elbName="demo-app-elb-prod"
AMI_ID=${1}
```

A couple of helper functions:

```
function techo() {
  echo "[$(date +%s)] " ${1}
}

function Err() {
  techo "ERR: ${1}"
  exit 100
}
```

Namely, the `techo` (timestamped echo) for a more informative output and `ERR` for when we encounter problems.

If we need to abort a deployment and restore our infrastructure to its original state, we will use this:

```
function rollback() {
  techo "Metrics check failed, rolling back"
  aws autoscaling update-auto-scaling-group --auto-scaling-group-name
```

```
${newActiveGroup} \
  --min-size 0
  techo "Instances ${1} entering standby in group ${newActiveGroup}"
  aws autoscaling enter-standby --should-decrement-desired-capacity \
    --auto-scaling-group-name ${newActiveGroup} --instance-ids ${1}
  techo "Detaching ${elbName} from ${newActiveGroup}"
  aws autoscaling detach-load-balancers --auto-scaling-group-name
${newActiveGroup} \
    --load-balancer-names ${elbName}
  Err "Deployment rolled back. Please check instances in StandBy."
}
```

In our case, we would abort if we detect an increase in the error count of certain metrics. We would put the newly deployed instances in **Standby** mode then detach the ELB from the given Auto Scaling Group.

Every time we launch new instances, we should pause to allow those to fully initialize then verify what they have done so far and the following `wait_for_instances()` function will help us with this task.

Wait for the expected number of instances to launch:

```
techo ">>> Waiting for instances to launch"
asgInstances=()

while [ ${#asgInstances[*]} -ne ${1} ];do
  sleep 10
  asgInstances=($(aws autoscaling describe-auto-scaling-groups \
    --auto-scaling-group-name ${newActiveGroup} | jq
.AutoScalingGroups[0].Instances[].InstanceId | tr -d '"' ))
  techo "Launched ${#asgInstances[*]} out of ${1}"
done
```

Wait for them to become available:

```
techo ">>> Waiting for instances to become available"
asgInstancesReady=0
iterList=(${asgInstances[*]})

while [ ${asgInstancesReady} -ne ${#asgInstances[*]} ];do
  sleep 10
  for i in ${iterList[*]};do
    asgInstanceState=$(aws autoscaling describe-auto-scaling-instances \
      --instance-ids ${i} | jq .AutoScalingInstances[0].LifecycleState | tr
-d '"')

    if [[ ${asgInstanceState} == "InService" ]];then
      asgInstancesReady="$((asgInstancesReady+1))"
```

```
        iterList=(${asgInstances[*]/${i}/})
    fi
  done
  techo "Available ${asgInstancesReady} out of ${#asgInstances[*]}"
done
```

Let the ELB declare them `InService`:

```
techo ">>> Waiting for ELB instances to become InService"
elbInstancesReady=0
iterList=(${asgInstances[*]})

while [ ${elbInstancesReady} -ne ${#asgInstances[*]} ];do
  sleep 10
  for i in ${iterList[*]};do
    elbInstanceState=$(aws elb describe-instance-health \
      --load-balancer-name ${elbName} --instances ${i} | jq
.InstanceStates[].State | tr -d '"')

    if [[ ${elbInstanceState} == "InService" ]];then
      elbInstancesReady=$((elbInstancesReady+1))
      iterList=(${asgInstances[*]/${i}/})
    fi
  done
  techo "InService ${elbInstancesReady} out of ${#asgInstances[*]}"
done
```

Next, since we know the region we will be working with, we set it in advance to avoid having to append it to each AWS CLI command:

```
export AWS_DEFAULT_REGION="us-east-1"
```

Before going any further, we make sure that there is a valid AMI ID to work with:

```
[[ ${AMI_ID} = ami-* ]] || Err "AMI ID ${AMI_ID} is invalid"
```

We will be working with two Auto Scaling Groups and one ELB, we check the properties of each group and extract the ELB name:

```
blueElb=$(aws autoscaling describe-auto-scaling-groups --auto-scaling-
group-names ${blueGroup} | \
  jq .AutoScalingGroups[0].LoadBalancerNames[0] | tr -d '"')
greenElb=$(aws autoscaling describe-auto-scaling-groups --auto-scaling-
group-names ${greenGroup} | \
  jq .AutoScalingGroups[0].LoadBalancerNames[0] | tr -d '"')
```

Next, we ensure that only one of the groups has the Production ELB associated with it:

```
[[ "${blueElb}" != "${greenElb}" ]] || Err "Identical ELB value for both
groups"

if [[ "${blueElb}" == "${elbName}" ]]; then
  activeGroup=${blueGroup}
  newActiveGroup=${greenGroup}
elif [[ "${greenElb}" == "${elbName}" ]]; then
  activeGroup=${greenGroup}
  newActiveGroup=${blueGroup}
fi

[ -n "${activeGroup}" ] || Err "Missing activeGroup"
[ -n "${newActiveGroup}" ] || Err "Missing newActiveGroup"

techo "Active group: ${activeGroup}"
techo "New active group: ${newActiveGroup}"
```

At this point, we have established which of the two groups is currently serving traffic (`Active`) and the one to take over from it (`newActive`).

Ideally, the `newActive` will be empty, before we deploy any instances within it:

```
asgInstances=($(aws autoscaling describe-auto-scaling-groups \
    --auto-scaling-group-name ${newActiveGroup} | jq
.AutoScalingGroups[0].Instances[].InstanceId | tr -d '"' ))
[ ${#asgInstances[*]} -eq 0 ] || Err "Found instances attached to
${newActiveGroup}!"
```

If that is so, we can proceed to get some stats from the `Active` group:

```
activeDesired=$(aws autoscaling describe-auto-scaling-groups \
    --auto-scaling-group-name ${activeGroup} | jq
.AutoScalingGroups[0].DesiredCapacity)
activeMin=$(aws autoscaling describe-auto-scaling-groups \
    --auto-scaling-group-name ${activeGroup} | jq
.AutoScalingGroups[0].MinSize)
activeMax=$(aws autoscaling describe-auto-scaling-groups \
    --auto-scaling-group-name ${activeGroup} | jq
.AutoScalingGroups[0].MaxSize)
scaleStep=$(( (30 * ${activeDesired}) /100 ))
```

`Desired/Min/Max` are the standard Auto Scaling values that we will end up transferring onto the `newActive` group. The `scaleStep`, in this case, 30% of the instances presumably in service, is the initial number of instances we would like to introduce (allowing them to receive live traffic) during the deployment.

It would be rather strange if our `Active` group is empty, otherwise should it have a low count, we round up the `scaleStep` to at least 1:

```
[ ${activeDesired} -gt 0 ] || Err "Active group ${activeGroup} is set to 0
instances!"

[ ${scaleStep} -gt 0 ] || scaleStep=1
```

Those were the prerequisites; now let us start the deployment by slowly scaling up the `newActive` group.

We would need a launch configuration. To create one, we can either pass all needed parameters ourselves or let EC2 copy most of those by providing an example instance from our `Active` group:

```
activeInstance=$(aws autoscaling describe-auto-scaling-groups \
  --auto-scaling-group-name ${activeGroup} | jq
.AutoScalingGroups[0].Instances[0].InstanceId | tr -d '"')

[[ ${activeInstance} = i-* ]] || Err "activeInstance ${activeInstance} is
invalid"

launchConf="demo-app-${AMI_ID}-$(date +%s)"

aws autoscaling create-launch-configuration --launch-configuration-name
${launchConf} \
  --image-id ${AMI_ID} --instance-id ${activeInstance}
```

Attach the newly created launch configuration to the group as follows:

```
techo ">>> Attaching ${launchConf} to ${newActiveGroup}"
aws autoscaling update-auto-scaling-group --auto-scaling-group-name
${newActiveGroup} \
  --launch-configuration-name ${launchConf}
```

Add ELB as follows:

```
techo ">>> Attaching ${elbName} to ${newActiveGroup}"
aws autoscaling attach-load-balancers --auto-scaling-group-name
${newActiveGroup} \
  --load-balancer-names ${elbName}
```

Start scaling up as follows:

```
techo ">>> Increasing ${newActiveGroup} capacity (min/max/desired) to
${scaleStep}"
aws autoscaling update-auto-scaling-group --auto-scaling-group-name
${newActiveGroup} \
  --min-size ${scaleStep} --max-size ${scaleStep} --desired-capacity
${scaleStep}
```

Wait for a moment or two, for the instances to boot:

```
wait_for_instances ${scaleStep}
```

Our initial batch of instances should now have been deployed, attached to the Production ELB, and started serving traffic. Before we launch even more copies of the new AMI, we ought to check that we have not caused any issues so far. One way to do this is to pause the deployment for a few minutes and examine metrics, such as number of non-200 responses, exceptions, or requests per second. For simplicity, in this example, we assume that this has been done; in real life, you would query your monitoring system(s) or perhaps pull samples of CloudWatch ELB/EC2 statistics.

If we do not detect any anomalies, we scale the newActive group further to match the size of the Active one:

```
techo ">>> Checking error metrics"
sleep 5
doRollback=false
${doRollback} && rollback "${asgInstances[*]}"

techo ">>> Matching ${newActiveGroup} capacity (min/max/desired) to that of
${activeGroup}"
aws autoscaling update-auto-scaling-group --auto-scaling-group-name
${newActiveGroup} \
  --min-size ${activeMin} --max-size ${activeMax} --desired-capacity
${activeDesired}
```

As you would expect, another check is in order:

```
wait_for_instances ${activeDesired}
```

This time, we could simulate a problem and trigger a rollback:

```
techo ">>> Checking error metrics"
sleep 5
doRollback=true
${doRollback} && rollback "${asgInstances[*]}"
```

The `rollback` function should take care of the rest. If we keep `doRollback` as `false`, our deployment continues as planned and we shift traffic completely from the `Active` to the `newActive` group by scaling the former down:

```
techo ">>> Reducing ${activeGroup} size to 0"
aws autoscaling update-auto-scaling-group --auto-scaling-group-name
${activeGroup} \
   --min-size 0 --max-size 0 --desired-capacity 0
```

And detach ELB from it:

```
techo ">>> Detaching ${elbName} from ${activeGroup}"
aws autoscaling detach-load-balancers --auto-scaling-group-name
${activeGroup} \
   --load-balancer-names ${elbName}
```

Now, let us see our script in action. First, we should simulate an `Active` group by manually scaling up, say the blue one, and attach the Production ELB to it:

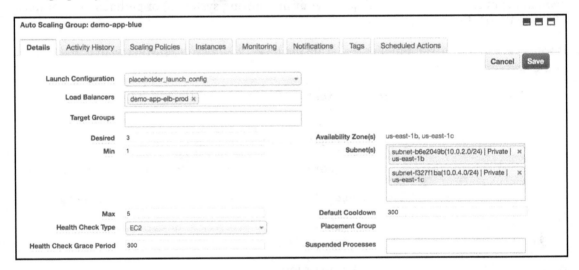

In a few moments, you should have three instances and ELB in blue:

Now, let us re-enable SCM polling for the `demo-app` job and trigger a run by pushing a code change to its CodeCommit repo. You should see the pipeline running, invoking the two downstream ones along the way.

If you choose to simulate a metrics problem and cause a rollback, then the deployed instances should end up in the **Standby** mode:

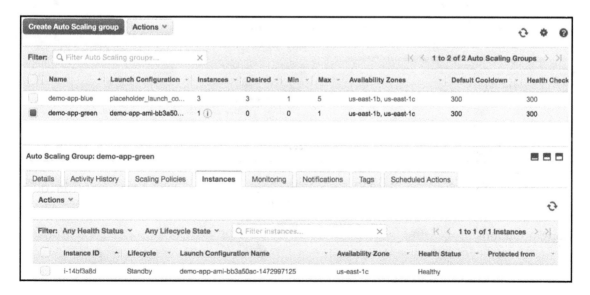

In this case, the `rollback` was triggered after the initial deployment of one instance (`scaleStep=1`). Theoretically, the next step would be to investigate the instance looking for a possible cause for the error metrics.

If the instance is deemed healthy, then we would need to complete the deployment manually by bringing the instance into service, scaling the group up further, then scaling the other group down (essentially completing the remaining steps in the `cdeployment` script).

Otherwise, the instance can be put into service, then the group scaled down to zero, bringing the infrastructure back to its original state with the blue group remaining as `Active`.

Should you have chosen not to cause any rollbacks, the deployment ought to proceed as planned and in the end the green group would have taken over the blue one, indicating a successful deployment:

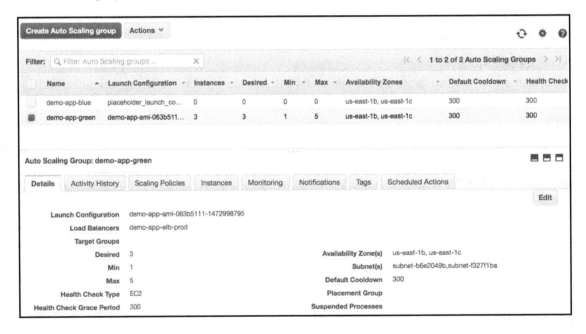

At this point, if you load the ELB URI in your browser, you should get a response from our `demo-app` as served from the newly deployed AMI.

Congratulations!

Summary

In this chapter, we finalized our Jenkins CI solution by adding the Deployment component to it. We made extensive use of the AWS CLI to orchestrate a blue/green deployment process. The resulting pipeline or a collection of such allows us to continuously integrate our application's code changes and build an AMI containing those, which is then deployed to a given environment after certain tests have been passed and criteria met.

The next chapter takes us in a new direction, introducing the topic of monitoring, metrics, and log collection. We will take a look at tools that can help us stay aware of the state of our infrastructure at any given time, visualize performance, and react to issues.

7
Metrics, Log Collection, and Monitoring

That's it. This chapter could well have ended here but I shall carry on for the benefit of those amongst us who would prefer things in more detail.

A great deal of the DevOps practice(s) evolve around the idea of being able to review and react to the state of your infrastructure at any given time – should you need to.

That is not to say, setup e-mail notifications for every time the date changes on your host, but a stream of sensible, usable amount of event data which would allow an operator to make a reasonably informed decision under stress and/or uncertainy.

If you have been paying attention in life so far, you would have noticed many a wise man talking about *balance, the golden middle.*

You should aim to configure your monitoring system in a way that you are notified of events of potential interest and in a timely manner. The notifications should arrive in a format that is hard to overlook, and should provide enough detail for an operator to be able to make an informed guess at what is going on.

At the same time, the said monitoring system must cause the least amount of alert fatigue (as outlined in this concise Datadog article: `https://www.datadoghq.com/blog/monitoring-101-alerting`).

Unfortunately for our friendship, finding that middle ground which suits your case (your infrastructure and the people looking after it) is an adventure which you will have to go on alone. We could however spend some quality time together, discussing a few of the tools that could make it even more enjoyable!

Checklists are sophisticated, so here is one:

- **Centralized logging**:
    - Ingesting and storing logs with **Logstash** and **Elasticsearch**
    - Collecting logs with Elasticsearch **Filebeat**
    - Visualizing logs with **Kibana**

- **Metrics**:
    - Ingesting and storing metrics with **Prometheus**
    - Gathering OS and application metrics with **Telegraf**
    - Visualizing metrics with **Grafana**

- **Monitoring**:
    - Alerting with **Prometheus**
    - Self-remediation with **Prometheus** and **Jenkins**

Naturally, we would require a few hosts to form our playground for all of the preceding checklist. There has been sufficient practice in deploying VPC EC2 instances on AWS in previous chapters, thus I hereby exercise the great power of delegation and assume the existence of:

- A VPC with an IGW, NAT gateway, 2x private and 2x public subnets
- 2x standalone, vanilla Amazon Linux EC2 instances (say `t2.small`) within the public subnets
- 1x Auto Scale Group (`t2.nano`) within the private subnets
- 1x Internet-facing ELB passing HTTP traffic to the Auto Scale Group

Centralized logging

Since the olden days, mankind has strived to use its limited attention span only on what really matters in life, and without having to look for it too hard – if possible. So we started with copying log files around, evolution brought us centralized (r)syslog and today (we learn from our mistakes) we have Logstash and Elasticsearch.

> *Elasticsearch is a distributed, open source search and analytics engine, designed for horizontal scalability, reliability, and easy management. It combines the speed of search with the power of analytics via a sophisticated, developer-friendly query language covering structured, unstructured, and time-series data.*
>
> *Logstash is a flexible, open source data collection, enrichment, and transportation pipeline. With connectors to common infrastructure for easy integration, Logstash is designed to efficiently process a growing list of log, event, and unstructured data sources for distribution into a variety of outputs, including Elasticsearch.*
>
> —https://www.elastic.co/products

Ingesting and storing logs with Logstash and Elasticsearch

We will be using Logstash to receive, process and then store log events into Elasticsearch.

For the purposes of the demos in this chapter, we'll be installing and configuring services manually, directly on the hosts. When done experimenting, you should, of course, use configuration management instead (wink).

Let us start by installing the two services on one of the standalone EC2 instances (we shall call it ELK):

```
# yum -y install
https://download.elastic.co/elasticsearch/release/org/elasticsearch/distrib
ution/rpm/elasticsearch/2.4.1/elasticsearch-2.4.1.rpm
https://download.elastic.co/logstash/logstash/packages/centos/logstash-2.4.
0.noarch.rpm
```

Edit /etc/elasticsearch/elasticsearch.yml:

> Please refer to:
> https://github.com/PacktPublishing/Implementing-DevOps-on-AWS
> /blob/master/5585_07_CodeFiles/elk/etc/elasticsearch/elasticse
> arch.yml

```
cluster.name: wonga-bonga
index.number_of_shards: 1
index.number_of_replicas: 0
index :
  refresh_interval: 5s
```

It is important to select a unique name for the Elasticsearch cluster, so that the node does not join somebody else's inadvertently, should there be any on your LAN. For development, we only ask for a single shard and no replicas. Impatience dictates a five second refresh rate on any ES indices.

Create a Logstash `patterns` folder:

 # mkdir /opt/logstash/patterns

Create a sample NGINX pattern `/opt/logstash/patterns/nginx` (ref: `https://www.digitalocean.com/community/tutorials/adding-logstash-filters-to-imp rove-centralized-logging`):

> **Please refer to:**
> `https://github.com/PacktPublishing/Implementing-DevOps-on-AWS /blob/master/5585_07_CodeFiles/elk/opt/logstash/patterns/nginx`

```
NGUSERNAME [a-zA-Z\.\@\-\+_%]+
NGUSER %{NGUSERNAME}
NGINXACCESS %{IPORHOST:clientip} %{NGUSER:ident} %{NGUSER:auth}
\[%{HTTPDATE:timestamp}\] "%{WORD:verb} %{URIPATHPARAM:request}
HTTP/%{NUMBER:httpversion}" %{NUMBER:response} (?:%{NUMBER:bytes}|-)
(?:"(?:%{URI:referrer}|-)"|%{QS:referrer}) %{QS:agent}
```

Create `/etc/logstash/conf.d/main.conf`:

> **Please refer to:**
> `https://github.com/PacktPublishing/Implementing-DevOps-on-AWS /blob/master/5585_07_CodeFiles/elk/etc/logstash/conf.d/main.co nf`

```
input {
  beats {
    port => 5044
  }
}

filter {
  if [type] == "nginx-access" {
    grok {
```

```
        match => { "message" => "%{NGINXACCESS}" }
    }
  }
}

output {
  elasticsearch {
    hosts => "localhost:9200"
    manage_template => false
    index => "%{[@metadata][beat]}-%{+YYYY.MM.dd}"
    document_type => "%{[@metadata][type]}"
  }
}
```

Logstash allows us to configure one or more listeners (inputs) in order to receive data, filters to help us process it and outputs specifying where that data should be forwarded once processed.

We expect logs to be delivered by Elasticsearch Filebeat on TCP: 5044. If the log event happens to be of type nginx-access, we have it modified according to the NGINXACCESS pattern then shipped to Elasticsearch on localhost TCP: 9200 for storage.

Finally, let us start the services:

```
# service elasticsearch start
# service logstash start
```

Collecting logs with Elasticsearch Filebeat

We have the systems in place; let us push somes from the ELK node that we are on.

We will use Filebeat to collect local logs of interest and forward those to Logstash (incidentally also local in this case):

> *Filebeat is a log data shipper. Installed as an agent on your servers, Filebeat monitors the log directories or specific log files, tails the files, and forwards them either to Elasticsearch or Logstash for indexing.*
> *– https://www.elastic.co/guide/en/beats/filebeat/current/filebeat-overview.html*

Installation:

```
# yum -y install
https://download.elastic.co/beats/filebeat/filebeat-1.3.1-x86_64.rpm
```

While functionality is provided to ship directly to ES, we are planning to use Logstash so we need to disable the Elasticsearch output and enable the logstash one in `/etc/filebeat/filebeat.yml`:

Please refer to:
https://github.com/PacktPublishing/Implementing-DevOps-on-AWS
/blob/master/5585_07_CodeFiles/elk/etc/filebeat/filebeat.yml

```
output:
  #elasticsearch:
  #  hosts: ["localhost:9200"]
  logstash:
    hosts: ["localhost:5044"]
```

We could also list a few more log files to collect:

```
filebeat:
  prospectors:
    -
      paths:
    - /var/log/*.log
        - /var/log/messages
        - /var/log/secure
```

Then start the service:

```
# service filebeat start
```

Fun, but let us launch a few other EC2 instances for even more of it!

We shall use the Auto Scale Group we mentioned earlier. We will install Filebeat on each instance and configure it to forward selected logs to our Logstash node.

First, ensure that the security group of the Logstash instance allows inbound connections from the Auto Scale Group (`TCP: 5044`).

Next, we use an EC2 User Data script to bootstrap the Filebeat binary and configuration onto each of the EC2 instances in our Auto Scale Group (we will call them webservers):

Please refer to:
https://github.com/PacktPublishing/Implementing-DevOps-on-AWS
/blob/master/5585_07_CodeFiles/webserver/user_data.sh

```
#!/bin/bash

yum -y install
https://download.elastic.co/beats/filebeat/filebeat-1.3.1-x86_64.rpm
yum -y install nginx

cat << EOF > /etc/filebeat/filebeat.yml
filebeat:
  prospectors:
    -

      paths:
        - /var/log/*.log
        - /var/log/messages
        - /var/log/secure

    -

      paths:
        - /var/log/nginx/access.log
      document_type: nginx-access
  registry_file: /var/lib/filebeat/registry
output:
  logstash:
    hosts: ["10.0.1.132:5044"]
EOF

service nginx start
service filebeat start
```

With that in place, go ahead and scale the group up. The new web server instances, should start streaming logs promptly.

Visualizing logs with Kibana

We have our logs collected by Filebeat and stored in Elasticsearch, how about browsing them?

Kibana, right on time:

> *Kibana is an open source analytics and visualization platform designed to work with Elasticsearch. You use Kibana to search, view, and interact with data stored in Elasticsearch indices. You can easily perform advanced data analysis and visualize your data in a variety of charts, tables, and maps.*
> *– https://www.elastic.co/guide/en/kibana/current/introduction.html*

Install the package:

```
# yum -y install
https://download.elastic.co/kibana/kibana/kibana-4.6.1-x86_64.rpm
```

Start the service:

```
# service kibana start
```

The default port is TCP:5601, if allowed in the relevant security group, you should be able to see the Kibana dashboard:

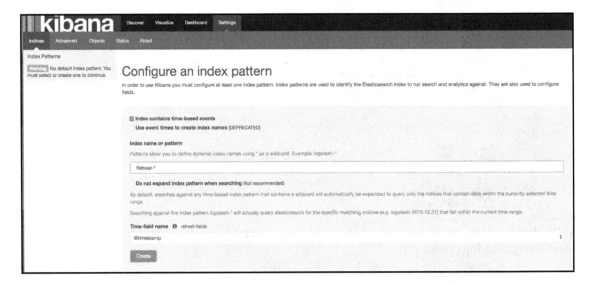

Set the **index pattern** to **filebeat-*** and click **Create**.

Kibana is now ready to display our Filebeat data. Switch to the **Discover** tab to see the list of recent events:

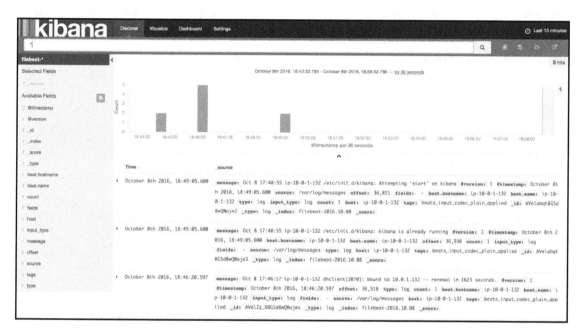

In addition to the standard **Syslog** messages, you will also notice some **NGINX access-log** entries, with various fields populated as per the filter we specified earlier:

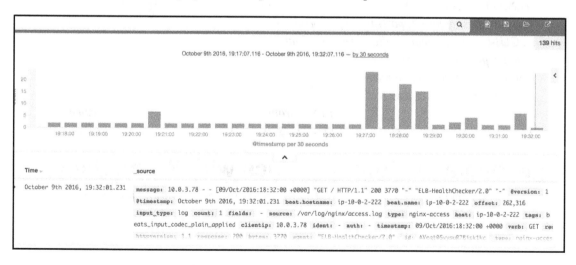

Logs: done. Now, how about some metrics?

Metrics

For ingesting, storing and alerting on our metrics, we shall explore another, quite popular open-source project called Prometheus:

Prometheus is an open-source systems monitoring and alerting toolkit originally built at SoundCloud.
Prometheus's main features are:
-a multi-dimensional data model (time series identified by metric name and key/value pairs)
— a flexible query language to leverage this dimensionality
— no reliance on distributed storage; single server nodes are autonomous
— time series collection happens via a pull model over HTTP
— pushing time series is supported via an intermediary gateway
— targets are discovered via service discovery or static configuration
— multiple modes of graphing and dashboarding support

—

https://prometheus.io/docs/introduction/overview/

Even though it is the kind of system that takes care of pretty much everything, the project still follows the popular UNIX philosophy of modular development. Prometheus is composed of multiple components, each providing a specific function:

— the main Prometheus server which scrapes and stores time series data
— client libraries for instrumenting application code
— a push gateway for supporting short-lived jobs
— a GUI-based dashboard builder based on Rails/SQL
— special-purpose exporters (for HAProxy, StatsD, Ganglia, etc.)
— an (experimental) alertmanager
— a command-line querying tool

— https://prometheus.io/docs/introduction/overview/

Ingesting and storing metrics with Prometheus

Our second EC2 instance is going to host the Prometheus service alongside Jenkins (we will come to that shortly), thus a rather appropriate name would be promjenkins.

As a start, download and extract Prometheus and Alertmanager in
`/opt/prometheus/server` and `/opt/prometheus/alertmanager` respectively (ref:
`https://prometheus.io/download`).

We create a basic configuration file for the Alertmanager in
`/opt/prometheus/alertmanager/alertmanager.yml` (replace e-mail addresses as
needed):

 Please refer to:
`https://github.com/PacktPublishing/Implementing-DevOps-on-AWS`
`/blob/master/5585_07_CodeFiles/promjenkins/opt/prometheus/aler`
`tmanager/alertmanager.yml`

```
global:
  smtp_smarthost: 'localhost:25'
  smtp_from: 'alertmanager@example.org'

route:
  group_by: ['alertname', 'cluster', 'service']
  group_wait: 30s
  group_interval: 5m
  repeat_interval: 1h
  receiver: team-X-mails

receivers:
- name: 'team-X-mails'
  e-mail_configs:
  - to: 'team-X+alerts@example.org'
    require_tls: false
```

This will simply e-mail out alert notifications.

Start the service:

```
# cd /opt/prometheus/alertmanager
# (./alertmanager 2>&1 | logger -t prometheus_alertmanager)&
```

Ensure the default TCP:9093 is allowed, then you should be able to get to the dashboard at
http://$public_IP_of_promjenkins_node:9093/#/status:

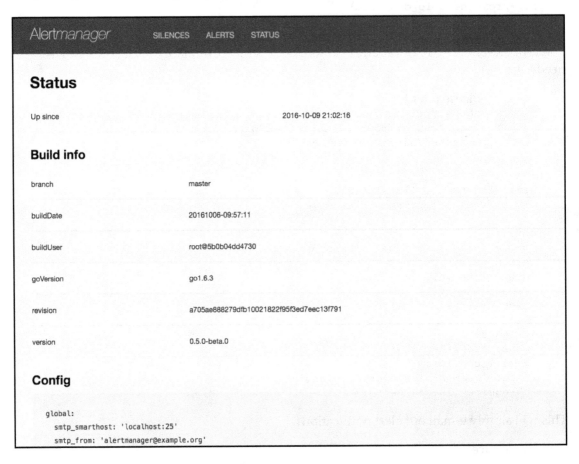

Back to the Prometheus server, the default /opt/prometheus/server/prometheus.yml
will suffice for now. We can start the service:

```
# cd /opt/prometheus/server
# (./prometheus -alertmanager.url=http://localhost:9093 2>&1 | logger -
t prometheus_server)
```

Open up `TCP:9090`, then try
`http://$public_IP_of_promjenkins_node:9090/status`:

| Prometheus | Alerts | Graph | Status ▾ | Help |

Runtime Information

| Uptime | 2016-10-09 20:14:44.970371246 +0000 UTC |

Build Information

Version	1.2.0
Revision	522c93361459686fe3687f5ffe68c2ee34ea5c8e
Branch	master
BuildUser	root@c8088ddaf2a8
BuildDate	20161007-12:53:55
GoVersion	go1.6.3

We are ready to start adding hosts to be monitored. That is to say targets for Prometheus to scrape.

Prometheus offers various ways in which targets can be defined. The one most suitable for our case is called `ec2_sd_config` (ref:
`https://prometheus.io/docs/operating/configuration/#<ec2_sd_config>`). All we need to do is provide a set of API keys with read-only EC2 access (**AmazonEC2ReadOnlyAccess** IAM policy) and Prometheus will do the host discovery for us (ref:
`https://www.robustperception.io/automatically-monitoring-ec2-instances`).

We append the `ec2_sd_config` settings to:
`/opt/prometheus/server/prometheus.yml`:

> Please refer to:
> `https://github.com/PacktPublishing/Implementing-DevOps-on-AWS`
> `/blob/master/5585_07_CodeFiles/promjenkins/opt/prometheus/serv`
> `er/prometheus.yml`

```
- job_name: 'ec2'
  ec2_sd_configs:
    - region: 'us-east-1'
      access_key: 'xxxx'
      secret_key: 'xxxx'
      port: 9126
```

```
relabel_configs:
  - source_labels: [__meta_ec2_tag_Name]
    regex: ^webserver
    action: keep
```

We are interested only in any instances in the `us-east-1` region with a name matching the `^webserver` regex expression.

Now let us bring some of those online.

Gathering OS and application metrics with Telegraf

We will be using the pull method of metric collection in Prometheus. This means that our clients (targets) will expose their metrics for Prometheus to scrape.

To expose OS metrics, we shall deploy InfluxData's Telegraf (ref: `https://github.com/influxdata/telegraf`).

It comes with a rich set of plugins, which will provide for a good deal of metrics. Should you need more, you have the option to write your own (in Go) or use the `exec` plugin which will essentially attempt to launch any type of script you point it at.

As for application metrics, we have two options (at least):

- Build a metrics API endpoint in the application itself
- Have the application submit metrics data to an external daemon (StatsD as an example)

Incidentally, Telegraf comes with a built-in StatsD listener, so if your applications already happen to have StatsD instrumentation, you should be able to simply point them at it.

Following on from the ELK example, we will extend the EC2 user data script to get Telegraf on our the Auto Scale Group instances.

 Please refer to:
`https://github.com/PacktPublishing/Implementing-DevOps-on-AWS`
`/blob/master/5585_07_CodeFiles/webserver/user_data.sh`

We append:

```
yum -y install
https://dl.influxdata.com/telegraf/releases/telegraf-1.0.1.x86_64.rpm

cat << EOF > /etc/telegraf/telegraf.conf
[global_tags]
[agent]
  interval = "10s"
  round_interval = true
  metric_batch_size = 1000
  metric_buffer_limit = 10000
  collection_jitter = "0s"
  flush_interval = "10s"
  flush_jitter = "0s"
  precision = ""
  debug = false
  quiet = false
  hostname = ""
  omit_hostname = false
[[outputs.prometheus_client]]
  listen = ":9126"
[[inputs.cpu]]
  percpu = true
  totalcpu = true
  fielddrop = ["time_*"]
[[inputs.disk]]
  ignore_fs = ["tmpfs", "devtmpfs"]
[[inputs.diskio]]
[[inputs.kernel]]
[[inputs.mem]]
[[inputs.processes]]
[[inputs.swap]]
[[inputs.system]]
EOF

service telegraf start
```

The important one here is `outputs.prometheus_client` with which we turn Telegraf into a Prometheus scrape target. By all means check the default configuration file if you'd like to enable more metrics during this test (ref:
`https://github.com/influxdata/telegraf/blob/master/etc/telegraf.conf`)

Next, check that TCP: `9126` is allowed into the Auto Scale Group security group, then launch a couple of nodes. In a few moments, you should see any matching instances listed in the targets dashboard (ref: `http://$` `public_IP_of_promjenkins_node:9090/targets`):

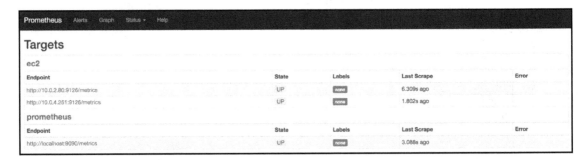

We see the new hosts under the **ec2** scrape job which we configured earlier.

Visualizing metrics with Grafana

It is true that Prometheus is perfectly capable of visualizing the data we are now collecting from our targets, as seen here:

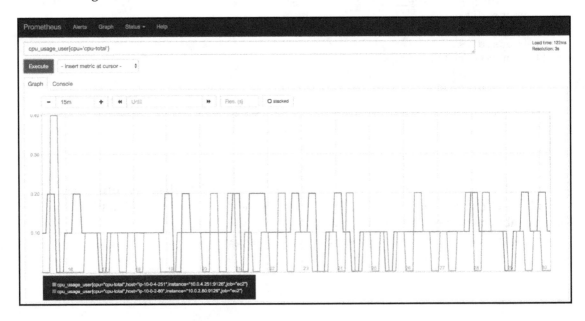

In fact, this is the recommended approach for any ad-hoc queries you might want to run.

Should you have an appetite for dashboards however, you would most certainly appreciate *Grafana – The 8th Wonder* (ref: `http://grafana.org`)

Check this out to get a feel for the thing: http://play.grafana.org

I mean, how many other projects do you know of with a *play* URL?!

1. So, yes, Grafana, let us install the service on the promjenkins node:

```
# yum -y install https://grafanarel.s3.amazonaws.com/builds/
  grafana-3.1.1-1470047149.x86_64.rpm
# service grafana-server start
```

The default Grafana port is TCP:3000, auth `admin:admin`. After updating the relevant security group, we should be able to see the screen at: `http://$ public_IP_of_promjenkins_node:3000`:

2. After logging in, first we need to create a **Data Sources** for our **Dashboards**:

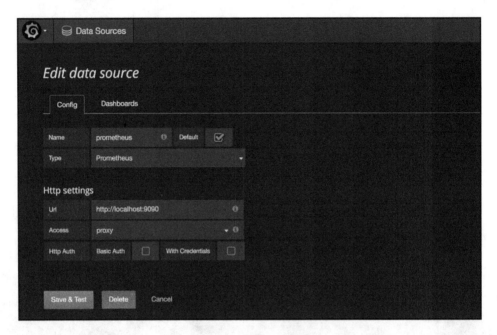

3. Back at the home screen, choose to create a new dashboard, then use the green button on the left to **Add Panel** then a **Graph**:

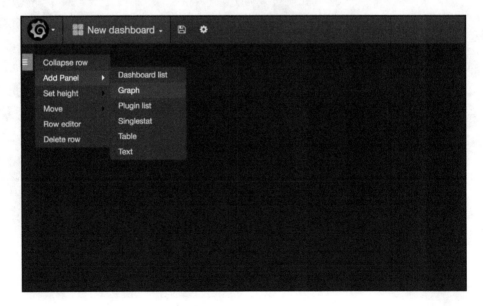

4. Then, adding a basic CPU usage plot looks like this:

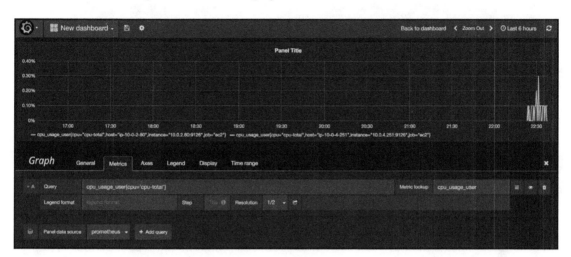

At this point I encourage you to browse `http://docs.grafana.org` to find out more about templating, dynamic dashboards, access control, tagging, scripting, playlist, and so on.

Monitoring

We have our metrics flowing into Prometheus. We also have a way of exploring and visualizing them. The next step should probably be to configure some sort of alerts, so that we show other people we are doing real work.

Alerting with Prometheus

ALERTING OVERVIEW
Alerting with Prometheus is separated into two parts. Alerting rules in Prometheus servers send alerts to an Alertmanager. The Alertmanager then manages those alerts, including silencing, inhibition, aggregation and sending out notifications via methods such as e-mail, PagerDuty and HipChat.
The main steps to setting up alerting and notifications are:
— Setup and configure the Alertmanager
— Configure Prometheus to talk to the Alertmanager with the-alertmanager.url flag
— Create alerting rules in Prometheus

— https://prometheus.io/docs/alerting/overview/

Let us break this down.

We already have Alertmanager running with some minimal configuration in
`/opt/prometheus/alertmanager/alertmanager.yml`.

Our Prometheus instance is aware of it as we passed the –
`alertmanager.url=http://localhost:9093` flag.

What is left is to create alerting rules. We'll store these in a `rules/` folder:

 # mkdir /opt/prometheus/server/rules

We need to tell Prometheus about this location, so we add a `rule_files` section to
`prometheus.yml`:

Please refer to:
`https://github.com/PacktPublishing/Implementing-DevOps-on-AWS`
`/blob/master/5585_07_CodeFiles/promjenkins/opt/prometheus/serv`
`er/prometheus.yml`

```
rule_files:
  - "rules/*.rules"
```

This way we can store separate rule files, perhaps based on the type of rules they contain?

As an example, let us have a keepalive and a disk usage alert:

Please refer to:
`https://github.com/PacktPublishing/Implementing-DevOps-on-AWS`
`/tree/master/5585_07_CodeFiles/promjenkins/opt/prometheus/serv`
`er/rules`

`/opt/prometheus/server/rules/keepalive.rules`:

```
ALERT Keepalive
  IF up == 0
  FOR 1m
  ANNOTATIONS {
     summary = "Instance {{$labels.instance}} down",
     description = "{{$labels.instance}} of job {{$labels.job}} has been
  down for more than 1 minute."
  }
```

`/opt/prometheus/server/rules/disk.rules`:

```
ALERT High_disk_space_usage
  IF disk_used_percent > 20
```

```
FOR 1m
ANNOTATIONS {
   summary = "High disk space usage on {{ $labels.instance }}",
   description = "{{ $labels.instance }} has a disk_used value of {{
$value }}% on {{ $labels.path }})",
   }
```

As you'll notice, we are being impatient with the FOR 1m and >20, meaning notifications will fire after just 60 seconds of alert detection and the alert threshold is only 20% of space used.

In a more realistic scenario, we should wait a bit longer to filter any transient issues and use severities to distinguish between critical alerts and warnings (ref: https://github.com/prometheus/alertmanager).

Reload Prometheus with the new rules in place. Now let us suppose that one of the web server nodes goes down:

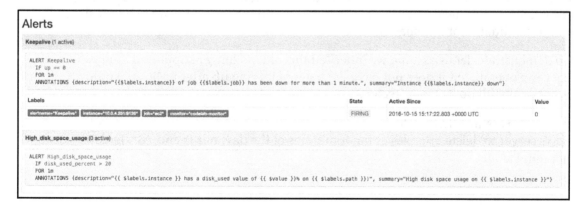

Switching to the **Alerts** tab we see:

In the Alertmanager respectively: (`http://$`
`public_IP_of_promjenkins_node:9093/#/alerts`):

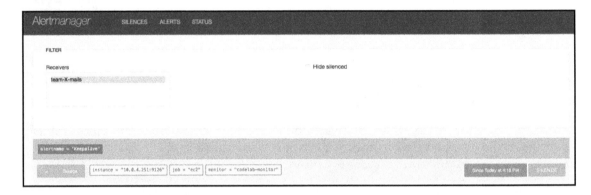

At this point an e-mail notification should have gone out as well.

Self-remediation with Prometheus and Jenkins

The dream of every operator is an ecosystem that looks after itself.

Imagine for a moment an environment in which, instead of receiving alerts prompting for action, we received mere notifications or reports of actions taken on our behalf.

For example, no more "CRITICAL: Service X is not responding. Please check." but "INFO: Service X was unresponsive at nn:nn:nn and was restarted after N seconds at nn:nn:nn" instead.

Well, technically, this should not be too difficult to achieve if we were to provide enough context to the tools we use today. It is not uncommon to find alerts which tend to get resolved in the same manner under the same conditions and those are to be considered prime candidates for automation.

To demonstrate, let us assume we inherited this old, no longer supported application. A cool app overall, but it does not have the habit of tidying up after itself, so would occasionally fill up its `tmp` directory.

Let us also assume that while we are not particularly excited about having to connect to this app's server to delete `tmp` files at random times of the day, our friend, Mr. Jenkins – does not mind at all.

Conveniently, Jenkins allows jobs to be triggered via a relevant `JOB_URL` and at the same time Prometheus supports webhook calls as a method of alert notification.

Here is the plan:

1. Prometheus will make a webhook call to Jenkins whenever a `disk_space` alert is fired with the alert details passed as parameters.
2. Jenkins will use the parameters to determine which host to connect to and clean up the application's `tmp` directory.

We would need to:

1. Create a parameterized Jenkins job which can be triggered remotely.
2. Allow Jenkins to `ssh` into the application's host.
3. Setup a webhook receiver in Prometheus which calls the Jenkins job when a certain alert is fired.

First a quick Jenkins installation onto our `promjenkins` node:

```
# yum install http://mirrors.jenkins-ci.org/redhat-stable/
  jenkins-2.7.1-1.1.noarch.rpm
# service jenkins start
```

`TCP:` `8080` needs to be open, then you should be able to reach the Jenkins service at `http://$public_IP_of_promjenkins_node:8080`.

Under **Manage Jenkins | Manage Users** create an account for Prometheus:

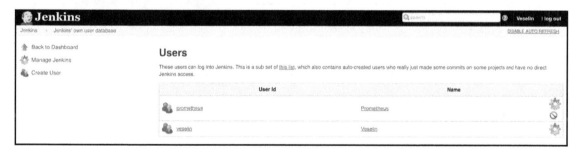

Then, under **Manage Jenkins | Configure Global Security**, select Jenkins' own user database and **Matrix-based Security**, then add both accounts.

Untick **Prevent Cross Site Request Forgery exploits** if you find that it causes issues when making `curl` request to Jenkins.

Grant yourself **Overall Administer rights** and **Prometheus Overall Read** plus **Job Build/Read**:

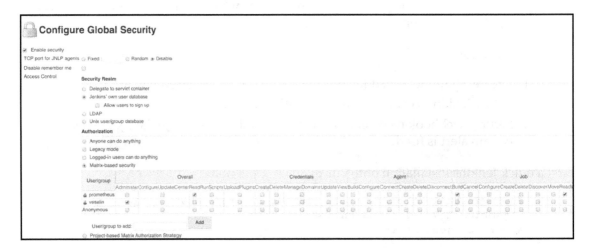

To be able to ssh into the app (web server) nodes we need a key for the Jenkins user:

```
# su - -s /bin/bash jenkins
$ ssh-keygen -trsa -b4096
Generating public/private rsa key pair.
Enter file in which to save the key (/var/lib/jenkins/.ssh/id_rsa):
Created directory '/var/lib/jenkins/.ssh'
...
```

While we are here, let us create an ssh config file for the Jenkins user (`~/.ssh/config`) containing:

```
Host 10.0.*
    StrictHostKeyChecking no
    UserKnownHostsFile=/dev/null
    User ec2-user
```

This is to allow our non-interactive jobs to ssh to instances for the first time.

We also need to take the generated public key and add it to the Auto Scale Group user data , so that it gets onto our web server instances. We will be using the standard (Amzn-Linux) ec2-user account to connect:

Please refer to:
`https://github.com/PacktPublishing/Implementing-DevOps-on-AWS`
`/blob/master/5585_07_CodeFiles/webserver/user_data.sh`

```
...
# Add Jenkins's key
cat << EOF >> /home/ec2-user/.ssh/authorized_keys
{{JENKINS_PUB_KEY_GOES_HERE}}
EOF
```

Now let us create the Jenkins job (freestyle project) with a few parameters:

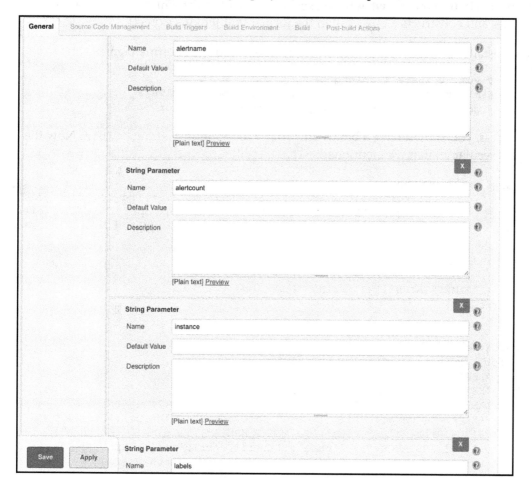

We will discuss those four parameters (`alertname`, `alertcount`, `instance`, `labels`) later. In the **Build** section, select **Execute shell** and enter `exit 0` as a placeholder until we are ready to configure the job further. **Save** and let's get back to Prometheus.

As we mentioned earlier, we will be using the webhook receiver to trigger the Jenkins job. While the receiver allows us to set a URL to call, it does not seem to allow for any parameters to be included. To accomplish this, we will use a small helper application called **prometheus-am-executor** (ref: `https://github.com/imgix/prometheus-am-executor`).

The executor sits between the Alertmanager and an arbitrary executable. It receives the webhook call from the Alertmanager and runs the executable, passing a list of alert variables to it. In our case, we will be executing a shell script which processes those variables and constructs a `curl` call in the format that Jenkins expects.

Let us install the helper app alongside Prometheus and the Alertmanager:

```
# yum -y install golang
# mkdir /opt/prometheus/executor && export GOPATH=$_
# go get github.com/imgix/prometheus-am-executor
```

On success, you should have a binary in `/opt/prometheus/executor/bin`. Now the script (executable) that we mentioned:

Please refer to:
`https://github.com/PacktPublishing/Implementing-DevOps-on-AWS`
`/blob/master/5585_07_CodeFiles/promjenkins/opt/prometheus/exec`
`utor/executor.sh`

```bash
#!/bin/bash

if [[ "$AMX_STATUS" != "firing" ]]; then
  exit 0
fi

main() {
  for i in $(seq 1 "$AMX_ALERT_LEN"); do
    ALERT_NAME=AMX_ALERT_${i}_LABEL_alertname
    INSTANCE=AMX_ALERT_${i}_LABEL_instance
    LABELS=$(set|egrep "^AMX_ALERT_${i}_LABEL_"|tr '\n' ' '|base64 -w0)
    PAYLOAD="{'parameter': [{'name':'alertcount', 'value':'${i}'},
{'name':'alertname', 'value':'${!ALERT_NAME}'}, {'name':'instance',
'value':'${!INSTANCE}'}, {'name':'labels', 'value':'${LABELS}'}]}"
    curl -s -X POST http://localhost:8080/job/prometheus_webhook/build --
user 'prometheus:password' --data-urlencode json="${PAYLOAD}"
  done
  wait
```

```
}

main "$@"
```

In essence we are constructing an HTTP call to our Jenkins job URL at `http://localhost:8080/job/prometheus_webhook/build` passing the `alertcount`, `alertname`, `instance` and `labels` parameters. All values come from the AMX environment variables which the prometheus-am-executor exposes (ref: `https://github.com/imgix/prometheus-am-executor`).

Now we need to reconfigure the Alertmanager to use webhooks:

 Please refer to:
`https://github.com/PacktPublishing/Implementing-DevOps-on-AWS /blob/master/5585_07_CodeFiles/promjenkins/opt/prometheus/aler tmanager/alertmanager.yml`

```
global:
  smtp_smarthost: 'localhost:25'
  smtp_from: 'alertmanager@example.org'

route:
  group_by: ['alertname', 'cluster', 'service']
  group_wait: 10s
  group_interval: 30s
  repeat_interval: 1m
  receiver: team-X-mails

  routes:
  - receiver: 'jenkins-webhook'
    match:
      alertname: "High_disk_space_usage"

receivers:
- name: 'team-X-mails'
  e-mail_configs:
  - to: 'veselin+testprom@kantsev.com'
    require_tls: false
    send_resolved: true

- name: 'jenkins-webhook'
  webhook_configs:
  - url: http://localhost:8888
```

So, we have added a new sub-route which would match on `alertname:`
`High_disk_space_usage` and use the `jenkins-webhook` receiver.

Reload Alertmanager and let us start the executor. Assuming that the `executor.sh` has
been placed in `/opt/prometheus/executor`:

```
# cd /opt/prometheus/executor
# ./bin/prometheus-am-executor -l ':8888' ./executor.sh
2016/10/16 17:57:36 Listening on :8888 and running [./executor.sh]
```

We have the executor running (port `8888`) and ready to accept requests from the
Alertmanager.

Before triggering any test alerts, let's go back to our Jenkins job. You are now familiar with
the parameters it expects and the ones that we pass via the `webhook | executor | jenkins`
setup that we have, so we can replace the contents of the placeholder **Build** step with this
shell script:

```
echo "alertname: ${alertname}"
echo "alertcount: ${alertcount}"
echo "instance: ${instance}"

export $(echo ${labels}|base64 -d)

NODE=$(echo ${instance}|cut -d: -f1)
LABEL_DIR=AMX_ALERT_${alertcount}_LABEL_path
APP_DIR='/opt/myapp/tmp'

if [ ${!LABEL_DIR} == ${APP_DIR} ];then
ssh ${NODE} "sudo rm -f ${APP_DIR}/*.tmp"
fi
```

To test all of this, we need to ssh into one of the ASG (web server) instances which
Prometheus is monitoring and setup a pretend App temporary folder like so:

```
# dd if=/dev/zero of=/tmp/dd.out bs=1M count=256
# mkfs.ext4 /tmp/dd.out
# mkdir -p /opt/myapp/tmp
# mount -oloop /tmp/dd.out /opt/myapp/tmp/
```

This should give us a small filesystem to play with. Next, we fill it up:

```
# dd if=/dev/zero of=/opt/myapp/tmp/dd.tmp bs=1M count=196
```

This is way over the 20% we have set in the `High_disk_space_usage` and should trigger it. In turn the executor should call Jenkins and run our job:

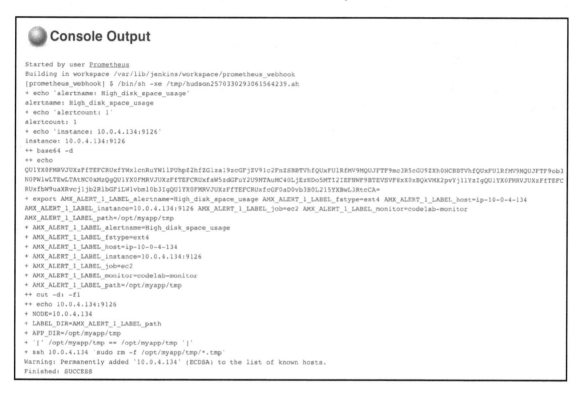

We can see Jenkins connecting to the affected instance over SSH, then clearing our fake application `tmp` directory.

It is important to note that while we allow ourselves root access for the purpose of this example, in any other circumstances you would either ensure that Jenkins could handle the given `tmp` directory as a non-privileged user, or if you would absolutely have to use `sudo` and then limit the commands and command line arguments that can be used.

Summary

In this chapter we looked at a way of centralizing our logs with Logstash and Elasticsearch then browsing them in Kibana. We configured a metrics collection and visualization with the help of Prometheus, Telegraf and Grafana. Finally, we added monitoring via Prometheus and self-remediation using Jenkins.

The next chapter takes us into the area of optimization. We shall discuss cost considerations and approaches to demand-based scaling.

8

Optimize for Scale and Cost

On the subject of optimization, we shall start from the top, that is to say the earliest stage: the design stage.

Imagine iterating over your architecture plan time and time again, until you have convinced yourself and your colleagues that this is the best you can do with the information available at that time. Now imagine that, unless you have a very unusual use case, other people have already done similar iterations and have kindly shared the outcome.

Back to reality and fortunately, we were not far off. There is indeed a collective AWS knowledge base in the form of blog posts, case studies, and white papers available to anybody embarking on their first cloud deployment.

We are going to take a distilled sample of that knowledge base and apply it to a common architecture example, in an attempt to achieve maximum scalability, whilst remaining cost efficient.

The example is going to be one of a typical frontend (NGINX nodes), backend (DB cluster) and a storage layer deployment within a VPC:

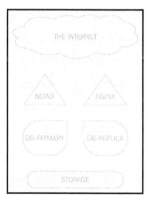

Whilst, technically, our whole deployment is on the Internet, the visual segregation above is to emphasize the network isolation properties of a VPC.

Architectural considerations

Let us now examine this deployment one component at a time, starting with the VPC itself.

The VPC

I am proceeding under the assumption that if you are still holding this book, you have likely accepted the way of the VPC.

CIDR

How many VPCs are you foreseeing having? Would they be linked (VPC peering) or would you be bridging other networks in (VPN)?

The answers to these questions play a role when choosing the CIDR for a VPC. As a general rule it is recommended to avoid common (household router) network addresses such as `192.168.1.0` or `10.0.0.0`.

Keep track of and assign different CIDRs if you have more than one VPC, even if you don't have an immediate need to peer them.

Consider a CIDR that will allow for large enough subnets to accommodate potential instance scaling with minimal fragmentation (number of subnets).

Subnets and Availability Zones

Availability Zones (**AZs**) are how we add resilience to a deployment, so we should have at least two of those. There might be configurations in which you have to use three, for example where a cluster quorum is needed, such as **ZooKeeper**. In that case, it is advisable to keep quorum members in separate zones in order to handle network partitions better. To accommodate this and to keep charges low, we could create subnets in three zones, deploy quorum clusters in all three, and other components (say **NGINX** hosts) in only two of those.

Let us illustrate an example where we have a Zookeeper and a web server (NGINX) component within our VPC. We have decided to use three AZs and maintain two sets of subnets: **public** and **private**. The former routing through the IGW, the latter via NAT:

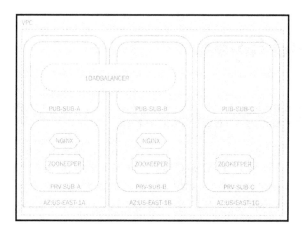

Here we have the ELB spanning across all three AZs and public subnets respectively. In the private subnet space, we find two web servers plus our cluster of three ZooKeeper nodes giving us a good balance of resilience at optimal cost.

VPC limits

AWS enforces certain initial limits on every account, which might catch you by surprise when your environment starts scaling up. Important ones to check are: **Instances**, **EBS** and **Networking** limits found on the **EC2 dashboard**:

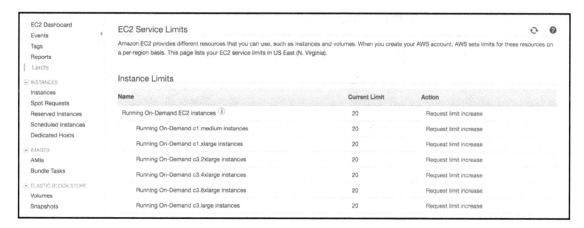

When requesting an increase, select a number that is high enough to provide a buffer for scaling, but not inadequately high as after all the limits are there to protect against accidental/erroneous overprovisioning.

The frontend layer

With the subnets in place, we can start thinking about our VPC inhabitants.

The frontend or application layer consists of our Auto Scaling Groups and the first decision that we'll face would be that of an EC2 instance type.

The profile of the frontend application would very much dictate the choice between a memory, compute or a storage optimized instance. With some help from fellow developers (in the case of an in-house application) and a suitable performance testing tool (or service) you should be able to ascertain which system resource does the given application make most use of.

Let us assume we have picked the **C4 Compute Optimized** instance class which AWS suggests for webservers. The next question will be – what size?

Well, one way to guess our way through, is to take the average number of requests per second that we would like to be able to support, deploy the minimum number of instances we can afford (two for resilience) of the smallest size available in the chosen class and run a load test against them. Ideally the average utilization across the two nodes would remain under 50% to allow for traffic spikes and events of failure where the remaining host takes all the load. If the results are far below that mark, then we should look for a different class with smaller instance types for better value. Otherwise we keep increasing the C4 size.

Next comes the question of Auto Scaling. We have the right class and instance size to work with, and now we need scaling thresholds. Firstly, if you are fortunate enough to have predicable loads, then your problems end here with the use of **Scheduled Actions**:

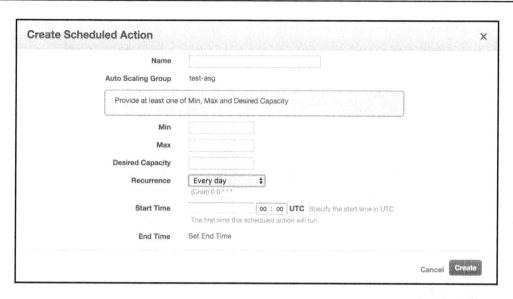

You can simply tell AWS scale me up at *X* o'clock then back down at *Y*. The rest of us, we have to set alarms and thresholds.

We've already decided that a 50% average utilization (let us say CPU) is our upper limit and by that time we should already have scaling in progress. Otherwise, if one of our two nodes fails, at that rate the other one will have to work at maximum capacity. As an example a **CloudWatch** alarm could be >40% average CPU used for five minutes, triggering an Auto Scaling Group action to increase the group size by 50% (which is one instance).

> In order to prevent unnecessary scaling events, it is important to adjust the value of the **Cooldown period**. It should reflect the expected time a newly launched instance will take to become fully operational and start affecting the **CloudWatch** metric.

For even finer control over how Auto Scaling reacts to the alarm we could use Step Scaling (ref: `http://docs.aws.amazon.com/autoscaling/latest/userguide/as-scale-based-on-deman d.html`). **Step Adjustments** allow for a varied response based on the severity of the threshold breach. For example, if the load increases from 40% to 50%, then scale up with only a single instance, but if the hop is from 40% to 70%, go straight to two or more.

> With Step Scaling the **Cooldown period** is set via the **Instance Warmup** option.

While we aim to scale up relatively quickly to prevent any service disruption, scaling down should be timely to save hourly charges, but not premature which could cause a scaling loop.

The **CloudWatch** alarm for scaling down should act over a much longer period of time than the five minutes we observed earlier. Also the gap between the threshold for scaling up and the one for scaling down should be wide enough not to have instances launch, only to be terminated shortly after.

EC2 Instance utilization is just one example of a trigger; it is also worth considering ELB metrics such as sum of total request, non-2XX responses or response latency. If you choose to use any of those, ensure that your scale down alarms react to the **INSUFFICIENT_DATA** state which is observed during periods of no traffic (perhaps late at night).

The backend layer

Behind the application we are likely to find a database cluster of some sort. For this example, we have chosen RDS (MySQL/PostgreSQL). However, the scaling and resilience ideas can be easily translated to suit a custom DB cluster on EC2 instances.

Starting with high-availability, in terms of RDS, the feature is called a **Multi-AZ** deployment. This gives us a Primary RDS instance with a hot **STANDBY** replica as a failover solution. Unfortunately, the Standby cannot be used for anything else, that is to say we cannot have it, for example, serving read-only queries.

A Multi-AZ setup within our VPC would look like this:

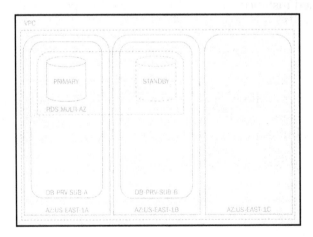

In the case of a **PRIMARY** outage, RDS automatically fails over to the **STANDBY**, updating relevant DNS records in the process. According to the documentation, a typical failover takes one to two minutes.

The triggers include the Primary becoming unavailable (thus failing AWS health-checks), a complete AZ outage, or a user interruption such as an RDS instance reboot.

So far, with Multi-AZ we have a reasonably resilient, but perhaps not very scalable setup. In a busy environment it is common to dedicate a primary DB node for writes, while reading is done off of replicas. The inexpensive option would be to add a single replica to our current arrangement:

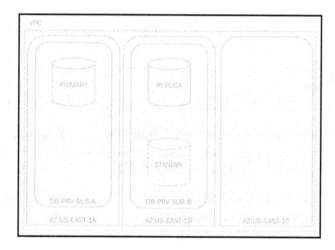

Here we write to **PRIMARY** and read from **REPLICA**, or for read-intensive applications reads can go to both.

If our budget allows, we can take this a step further and provide a **REPLICA** in both subnets in which we deploy frontend/application nodes:

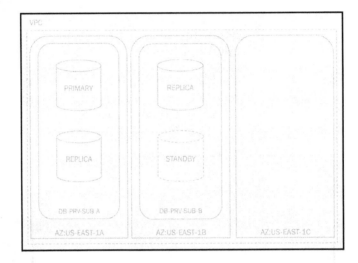

Latency across AWS zones is already pretty low, but with such a per-zone RDS distribution, we reduce it even further. All hosts would write to the **PRIMARY**. However they can assign a higher priority to their local (same zone) **REPLICA** when reading.

And since we are on a spending spree, additional RDS performance boost can be gained with provisioned IOPS. This is something to consider if you are running a heavy workload and in need of high RDS Storage I/O.

Although indirectly, caching is another very effective way to increase RDS scalability by alleviating the load.

Popular software choices here are **Memcached** and **Redis**. Either is simple to setup locally (on each application host). If you would like to benefit from a shared cache then you could run a cluster on EC2 or use the AWS managed ElastiCache service. With the latter, we can have again a **Multi-AZ** configuration plus multiple replicas for resilience and low-latency:

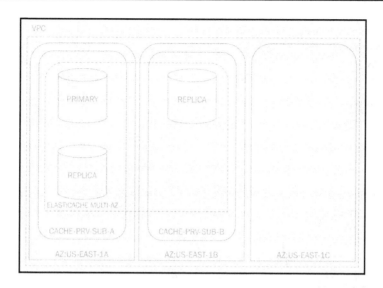

You will notice that the failover scenario differs from RDS in that there is no standby instance. In the event of a **PRIMARY** failure **ELASTICACHE** promotes the most up-to-date **REPLICA** instead.

> Note that after the promotion the **PRIMARY** endpoint remains the same, however the promoted Replica's address changes.

The object storage layer

In the effort of achieving effortless scalability, we must put emphasis on building stateless applications where possible. Not keeping state on our application nodes would mean storing any valuable data away from them. A classic example is **WordPress**, where user uploads are usually kept locally, making it difficult to scale such a setup horizontally.

While it is possible to have a shared file system across your EC2 instances using **Elastic File System** (**EFS**), for reliability and scalability we are much better off using an object storage solution such as **AWS S3**.

It is fair to say that accessing S3 objects is not as trivial as working with an EFS volume, however the AWS tools and SDKs lower the barrier considerably. For easy experimenting, you could start with the S3 CLI. Eventually you would want to build S3 capabilities into your application using one of the following:

- Java/.NET/PHP/Python/Ruby or other SDKs (ref:
  `https://aws.amazon.com/tools/`)
- REST API (ref:
  `http://docs.aws.amazon.com/AmazonS3/latest/dev/RESTAPI.html`)

In previous chapters we examined IAM Roles as a convenient way of granting S3 bucket access to EC2 instances. We can also enhance the connectivity between those instances and S3 using VPC Endpoints:

> *A VPC endpoint enables you to create a private connection between your VPC and another AWS service without requiring access over the Internet, through a NAT device, a VPN connection, or AWS Direct Connect. Endpoints are virtual devices. They are horizontally scaled, redundant, and highly available VPC components that allow communication between instances in your VPC and AWS services without imposing availability risks or bandwidth constraints on your network traffic.*
>
> – `http://docs.aws.amazon.com/AmazonVPC/latest/UserGuide/vpc-endpoints.html`

If you have clients in a different geographic location uploading content to your bucket, then S3 transfer acceleration (ref:
`http://docs.aws.amazon.com/AmazonS3/latest/dev/transfer-acceleration.html`) can be used to improve their experience. It is simply a matter of clicking **Enable** on the bucket's settings page:

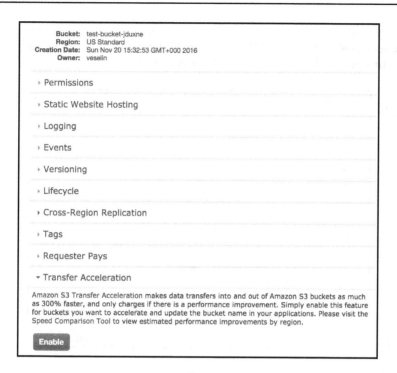

We have now covered speed improvements; scalability comes built into the S3 service itself and for cost optimization we have the different storage classes.

S3 currently supports four types (classes) of storage. The most expensive and most durable being the **Standard class**, which is also the default. This is followed by the **Infrequent Access class (Standard_IA)** which is cheaper, however keep in mind that it is indeed intended for rarely accessed objects otherwise the associated retrieval cost would be prohibitive. Next is the **Reduced Redundancy class** which, despite the scary name, is still pretty durable at 99.99%. And lastly, comes the **Glacier storage class** which is akin to a tape backup in that objects are archived and there is a 3-5 hour retrieval time (with 1-5 minute urgent retrievals available at a higher cost).

You can specify the storage class (except for Glacier) of an object at time of upload or change it retrospectively using the AWS console, CLI or SDK. Archiving to Glacier is done using a bucket lifecycle policy (bucket's settings page):

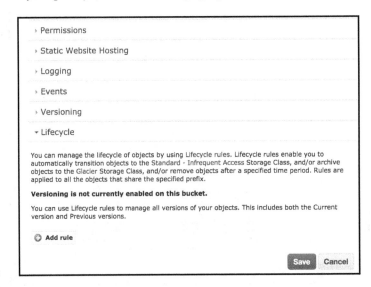

We need to add a new rule, describing the conditions under which an object gets archived:

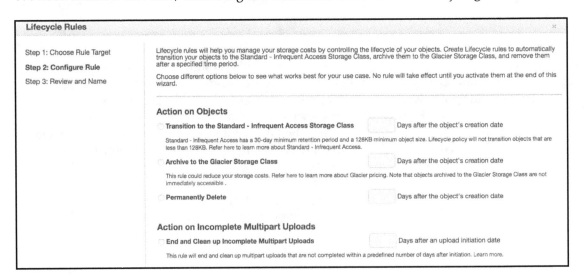

Incidentally, Lifecycle rules can also help you clean up old files.

The load balancing layer

The days of the *Wild Wild West* when one used to setup web servers with public IPs and DNS round-robin have faded away and the load balancer has taken over.

We are going to look at the AWS ELB service, but this is certainly not the only available option. As a matter of fact, if your use case is highly sensitive to latency or you observe frequent, short lived traffic surges then you might want to consider rolling your own EC2 fleet of load balancing nodes using NGINX or HAProxy.

The ELB service is priced at a flat per-hour fee plus bandwidth charges, so perhaps not much we can do to reduce costs, but we can explore ways of boosting performance.

Cross-zone load balancing

Under normal conditions, a Classic ELB would deploy its nodes within the zones which our backend (application) instances occupy and forward traffic according to those zones. That is to say, the ELB node in zone **A** will talk to the backend instance in the same zone, and the same principle applies for zone **B**:

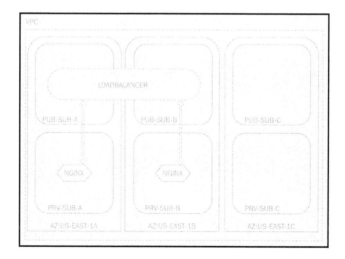

This is sensible as it clearly ensures lowest latency, but there are a couple of things to note:

- An equal number of backend nodes should be maintained in each zone for best load spread
- Clients caching the IP address for an ELB node would stick to the respective backend instance

To improve the situation at the expense of some (minimal) added latency, we can enable **Cross-Zone Load Balancing** in the Classic ELB's properties:

This will change the traffic distribution policy, so that requests to a given ELB node will be evenly spread across all registered (status: InService) backend instances, changing our earlier diagram to this:

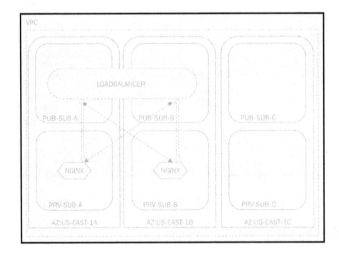

An unequal number of backend nodes per zone would no longer have an impact on load balancing, nor would external parties targeting a single ELB instance.

ELB pre-warming

An important aspect of the ELB service is that it runs across a cluster of EC2 instances of a given type, very much like our backend nodes. With that in mind, it should not come as a surprise that ELB scales based on demand, again much like our Auto Scaling Group does.

This is all very well when incoming traffic fluctuates within certain boundaries, so that it can be absorbed by the ELB or increases gradually, allowing enough time for the ELB to scale and accommodate. However, sharp surges can result in ELB dropping connections if large enough.

This can be prevented with a technique called **pre-warming** or essentially scaling up an ELB ahead of anticipated traffic spikes. Currently this is not something that can be done at the user end, meaning you would need to contact AWS Support with an ELB pre-warming request.

The CDN layer

CloudFront or AWS's CDN solution is yet another method of improving the performance of the ELB and S3 services. If you are not familiar with CDN networks, those, generally speaking, provide faster access to any clients you might have in a different geographic location from your deployment location. In addition, a CDN would also cache data so that subsequent requests won't even reach your server (also called **origin**) greatly reducing load.

So, given our VPC deployment in the US, if we were to setup a **CloudFront distribution** in front of our ELB and/or S3 bucket, then requests from clients originating in say Europe would be routed to the nearest *European CloudFront Point-of-Presence* which in turn would either serve a cached response or fetch the requested data from the ELB/S3 over a high-speed, internal AWS network.

To setup a basic **web distribution** we can use the **CloudFront dashboard**:

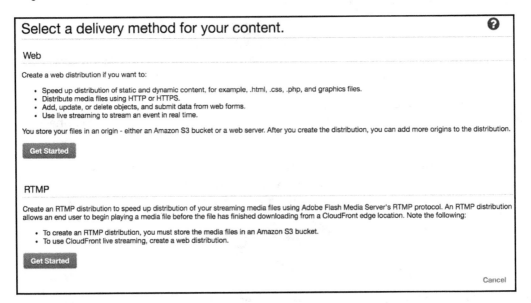

Once we **Get Started** then the second page presents the distribution properties:

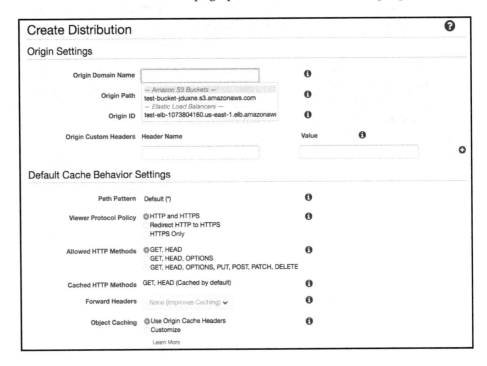

Conveniently, resources within the same AWS account are suggested. The origin is the source of data that CloudFront needs to talk to, for example the ELB sitting in front of our application. In the **Alternate Domain Names** field we would enter our website address (say `www.example.org`), the rest of the settings can remain with their defaults for now.

After the distribution becomes active all that is left to do is to update the DNS record for `www.example.org` currently pointing at the ELB to point to the distribution address instead.

Spot instances

Our last point is on making further EC2 cost savings using **Spot** instances. These represent unused resources across the EC2 platform, which users can bid on at any given time. Once a user has placed a winning bid and has been allocated the EC2 instance, it remains theirs for as long as the current Spot price stays below their bid, else it gets terminated (a notice is served via the instance meta-data, ref:
`http://docs.aws.amazon.com/AWSEC2/latest/UserGuide/spot-interruptions.html`).

These conditions make Spot instances ideal for workflows, where the job start time is flexible and any tasks can be safely resumed in case of instance termination. For example, one can run short-lived Jenkins jobs on Spot instances (there is even a plugin for this) or use it to run a workflow which performs a series of small tasks that save state regularly to S3/RDS.

AWS Calculators

Lastly, a simple yet helpful tool to give you an idea of how much your planned deployment would cost: `http://calculator.s3.amazonaws.com/index.html` (remember to untick the **FREE USAGE TIER** near the top of the page)

And if you were trying to compare the cost of on-premise to cloud, then this might be of interest: `https://aws.amazon.com/tco-calculator/`.

Summary

In this chapter we examined different ways in which to optimize both the scalability and running costs of an AWS deployment.

We started with the underlying VPC and its core properties such as the CIDR, subnets and how to plan for growth. We covered methods of improving the performance of the frontend, backend, storage and load balancing components. Then we looked at AWS Spot instances as a very cost efficient solution for executing lower-priority, batch processing jobs.

In the next chapter we move into the realm of security and explore the topic of how to better harden an AWS environment.

9
Secure Your AWS Environment

Security is unsurprisingly a very hot topic in *The Cloud Computing – should you be doing it?* debate.

On one side we have the *my-hardware-is-my-castle* group of people, who find it deeply unnatural to even think of delegating your compute environment to some abstract entity that assures you that you own the capacity of X number of machines at any given time, but which you cannot see or touch. Not to mention the question of your data.

On the other, we find the people who do not really mind the mystical concept of the cloud at all. Their main interest is in having instant access to somewhat unlimited amount of compute resources at a reasonable cost. Unfortunately, they might occasionally concentrate too much on getting a job done quickly, ignoring some valid, healthy concerns that the former group puts forward.

Then there is the middle ground – those of us who recognize the sacrifices one has to accept when moving to the cloud as well as the various solutions to make up for those. That is to say, with well-designed applications plus carefully planned-out architecture, your environment can remain adequately secure regardless of the underlying type of hosting platform.

We are going to examine a few of these solutions and practices in attempt to make our AWS environment more secure.

We shall cover:

- Managing access using IAM
- VPC security
- EC2 security
- Security auditing

Let us begin.

Managing access using IAM

> *AWS Identity and Access Management (IAM) is a web service that helps you securely control access to AWS resources for your users. You use IAM to control who can use your AWS resources (authentication) and what resources they can use and in what ways (authorization).*
> *ref:* http://docs.aws.amazon.com/IAM/latest/UserGuide/introduction.html

We will be using IAM for managing access (be it user or application) to services under our AWS account.

Securing the root account

When a new AWS account is opened, it comes with a single user (the account owner) also referred to as the **root login**. This almighty user has all the powers, including the option of terminating the AWS account. For this reason, it is often advised that the root login is only used for high-level account management purposes while any day-to-day operations are done via IAM user accounts.

We shall follow this recommendation, so the very first thing we do after registering an AWS account is to login as **root**, disable any unnecessary authentication mechanisms and create ourselves a lower-privileged IAM user account.

Let us browse to the AWS Console (ref: https://console.aws.amazon.com/console/home):

Notice the small print underneath the **Sign In** button. This is the link we need to follow in order to access the root account, which takes us to a slightly different login page as shown in the following screenshot:

Here, use your main Amazon credentials; you should see the familiar Console page. click on the name in the top-right corner:

Choosing **Security Credentials** takes us to our root account security options:

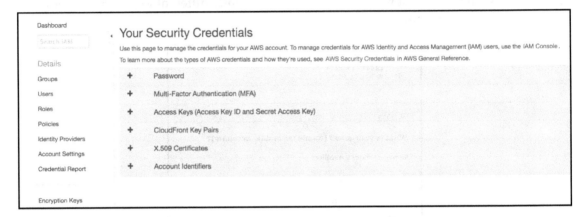

Enable **Multi-Factor Authentication (MFA);** there really isn't a good reason not to. You could purchase a hardware token device or simply use an app on your phone such as the **Google Authenticator**.

Delete the keys under **Access Keys**. These are used for API access, which you are very likely not going to need for account management tasks.

Next, click on the **Account Settings** link on the left, to update the current password policy. With the various password management tools available today, choosing a complex password and changing it often is no longer an inconvenience, so go crazy:

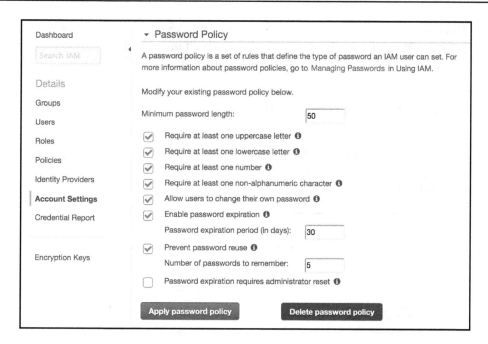

On the same page, we can disable any regions we are not going to be using:

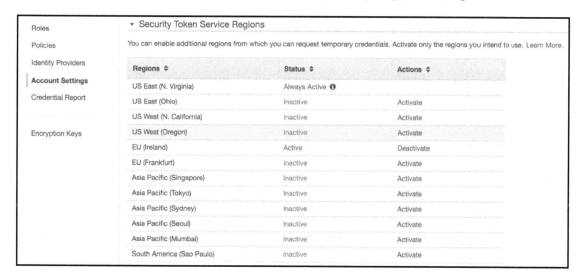

Now we proceed to create the IAM accounts for daily AWS usage. We will organize our users into groups. We start with a user in a group which has administrator privileges, which can then be used to manage almost all aspects of the AWS account.

On the left, select **Groups** and create a new group, granting it administrator access. Then under **Users**, create an account for yourself and make it a member of that group.

During the user creation process you would have had the option to create API access keys (you could also do it at a later stage too), which are useful if you are planning to use the AWS CLI or programmatic access in general. Once created, select the user and switch to the **Security Credentials** tab:

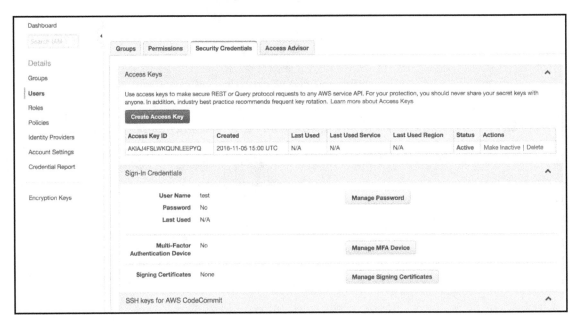

Here you have the option to create an **Access Keys** pair, if you did not do so earlier, as well as set a password for using the AWS Console. As mentioned earlier, you should take the opportunity to enable **MFA** (to take this a step further, have a look at http://docs.aws.amazon.com/IAM/latest/UserGuide/id_credentials_mfa_configure-api-require.html). Also if you are planning to use the CodeCommit service over SSH, this is where you upload your public key.

This is it, from now on you can login to the AWS Console using the username and password of the IAM account you just created, keeping the root for special occasions.

As a side note for those who might already maintain a user database external to AWS, there are ways to integrate it using **Federation**.

> For more details, see either of these links:
> `https://aws.amazon.com/iam/details/manage-federation`
> `http://docs.aws.amazon.com/IAM/latest/UserGuide/id_roles_provide`
> `rs.html`

VPC security

If you have deployed your resources in a VPC, you are already moving in the right direction. Here we are mostly going to concern ourselves with network security and the tools or features a VPC provides for enhancing it.

Security Groups

These represent our first layer of defense as stated in the AWS documentation. **Security Groups (SG)** get assigned to EC2 instances (generally speaking) and provide a type of stateful firewall, which supports allow rules only.

They are very flexible and an EC instance can have multiple such groups assigned to it. The rules can be based on host IP addresses, CIDRs or even on other Security Groups, for example, allow inbound `HTTP:80` from group ID `sg-12345`.

Usually, within a VPC we would create an SG per role, such as **web server**, **db**, **cache**. Instances of the same component would then be assigned the respective SG, thus regulating traffic between the different components of a platform.

> It is often tempting to allow traffic based on the VPC CIDR address, resting on the fact that the VPC is largely an isolated environment. Resist that as much as possible and limit access to components that actually need it.
> The db SG should allow traffic from/to the web server SG, but possibly not from the cache one.

Network ACLs

The second layer comes in the form of Network ACLs.

The ACLs are stateless, they apply to the underlying subnet that an instance lives in and their rules are evaluated based on priority, just like an old fashioned firewall. As a bonus, you can also set deny policies.

 Network ACLs sit at the edge of the VPC, hence are evaluated before traffic reaches any Security Groups. This feature plus the ability to set deny rules make them very suitable for reacting to potential DDOS threats.

Overall, both types of traffic management have their place in our VPC security design. ACLs should store a set of broader, less frequently changing rules, complemented by flexible Security Groups for fine-grained control.

VPN gateway

If it so happens that you are using a VPC as an extension to your on-premise infrastructure, it would make a lot of sense to have the two sides more tightly connected.

Instead of restricting external access via Security Groups or ACLs, you could create a secure VPN channel, benefiting from the implied encryption.

You can connect your VPC to your office network using either a hardware or a software VPN solution (ref: http://docs.aws.amazon.com/AmazonVPC/latest/UserGuide/vpn-connections.html).

For more demanding use-cases, one could even route their VPN traffic over a high-speed direct link to AWS using the AWS Direct Connect service (ref: http://docs.aws.amazon.com/directconnect/latest/UserGuide/Welcome.html).

VPC peering

In a similar situation, where instead of your office network you have another VPC which needs to communicate with your, let us call it primary one, you could use VPC peering:

> *A VPC peering connection is a networking connection between two VPCs that enables you to route traffic between them using private IP addresses. Instances in either VPC can communicate with each other as if they are within the same network. You can create a VPC peering connection between your own VPCs, or with a VPC in another AWS account within a single region.*
>
> *AWS uses the existing infrastructure of a VPC to create a VPC peering connection; it is neither a gateway nor a VPN connection, and does not rely on a separate piece of physical hardware. There is no single point of failure for communication or a bandwidth bottleneck.*
> *ref:*
> http://docs.aws.amazon.com/AmazonVPC/latest/PeeringGuide/vpc-peering-ov
> erview.html

Your VPCs will be able to communicate directly (within the same region) so you will not need to expose any services that do not explicitly need to be exposed. In addition, you can conveniently keep using private addresses for communication.

EC2 security

Diving deeper into our VPC, we are now going to look at ways to enhance the security around our EC2 instances.

IAM Roles

IAM EC2 Roles are the recommended way to grant your application access to AWS services.

As an example, let us assume we had a web app running on our web server EC2 instance and it needs to be able to upload assets to S3.

A quick way of satisfying that requirement would be to create a set of IAM access keys and hardcode those into the application or its configuration. This however means that from that moment on it might not be very easy to update those keys unless we perform an app/config deployment. Furthermore, we might for one reason or another end up re-using the same set of keys with other applications.

The security implications are evident: reusing keys increases our exposure if those get compromised and having them hardcoded greatly increases our reaction time (it takes more effort to rotate such keys).

An alternative to the preceding method would be to use Roles. We would create an EC2 Role, grant it write access to the S3 bucket and assign it to the web server EC2 instance. Once the instance has booted, it is given temporary credentials which can be found in its metadata and which get changed at regular intervals. We can now instruct our web app to retrieve the current set of credentials from the instance metadata and use those to carry out the S3 operations. If we were to use the AWS CLI on that instance, we would notice that it fetches the said metadata credentials by default.

 Roles can be associated with instances only at launch time, so it is a good habit to assign one to all your hosts even if they do not need it right away.

Roles can be used to assume other roles, making it possible for your instances to temporarily escalate their privileges by assuming a different role within your account or even across AWS accounts (ref: `http://docs.aws.amazon.com/STS/latest/APIReference/API_AssumeRole.html`).

SSH access

The most common way to interact with an EC2 instance would be over SSH. Here are a couple of ideas to make our SSH sessions even more secure.

Individual keys

When a vanilla EC2 instance is launched it usually has a set of PEM keys associated with it to allow initial SSH access. If you also work within a team, my recommendation would be not to share that same key pair with your colleagues.

Instead, as soon as you, or ideally your configuration management tool, gain access to the instance, individual user accounts should be created and public keys uploaded for the team members (plus `sudo` access where needed). Then the default `ec2-user` account (on Amazon Linux) and PEM key can be removed.

Entrypoint

Regardless of the purpose that an EC2 instance serves, it is rarely the case that you must have direct external SSH access to it.

Assigning public IP addresses and opening ports on EC2 instances is often an unnecessary exposure in the name of convenience and somewhat contradicts the idea of using a VPC in the first place.

SSH can unarguably be useful however. So, to maintain the balance between the forces, one could setup an SSH gateway host with a public address. You would then restrict access to it to your home and/or office network and permit SSH connections from that host towards the rest of the VPC estate.

The chosen node becomes the administrative entry point of the VPC.

ELBs everywhere

Latency is of importance. You will find brilliant engineering articles online from expert AWS users who have put time and effort into benchmarking ELB performance and side-effects.

Perhaps not surprisingly their findings show that there is a given latency penalty with using an ELB, as opposed to serving requests directly off of a backend web server farm. The other side to this however is the fact that such an additional layer, be it an ELB or a cluster of custom HAProxy instances, acts as a shield in front of those web servers.

With a balancer at the edge of the VPC, web server nodes can remain within the private subnet which is not a small advantage if you can afford the said latency trade-off.

HTTPS by default

Services like the **AWS Certificate Manager**, make using SSL/TLS encryption even easier and more affordable. You get the certificates plus automatic renewals for free (within AWS).

Whether traffic between an ELB and the backend instances within a VPC should be encrypted is another good question, but for now please do add a certificate to your ELBs and enforce HTTPS where possible.

Encrypted storage

Logically, since we are concerned with encrypting our HTTP traffic, we should not ignore our data at rest.

The most common type of storage on AWS must be the EBS volume with S3 right behind it. Each of the two services supports a strong and effortless implementation of encryption.

EBS volumes

First, it should be noted that not all EC2 instance types support encrypted volumes. Before going any further, please consult this table:

```
http://docs.aws.amazon.com/AWSEC2/latest/UserGuide/EBSEncryption.html#EBSEncryp
tion_supported_instances
```

Also, let us see what does get encrypted and how:

> *When you create an encrypted EBS volume and attach it to a supported instance type, the following types of data are encrypted:*
> *– Data at rest inside the volume*
> *– All data moving between the volume and the instance*
> *– All snapshots created from the volume*
> *The encryption occurs on the servers that host EC2 instances, providing encryption of data-in-transit from EC2 instances to EBS storage.*
> *ref:*
> ```
> http://docs.aws.amazon.com/AWSEC2/latest/UserGuide/EBSEncryption.html
> ```

Note that the data gets encrypted on the servers that host EC2 instances, that is to say the hypervisors.

Naturally, if you wanted to go the extra mile you could manage your own encryption on the instance itself. Otherwise, you can be reasonably at peace knowing that each volume gets encrypted with an individual key which is in turn encrypted by a master key associated with the given AWS account.

In terms of key management, AWS recommends that you create a custom key to replace the one which gets generated for you by default. Let us create a key and put it to use.

On the IAM dashboard, select **Encryption Keys** on the left:

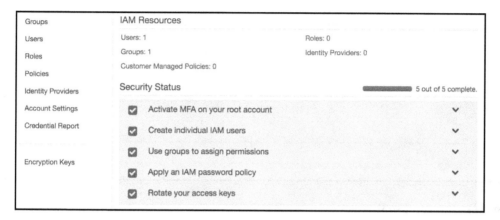

Choose to **Create Key** and fill in the details:

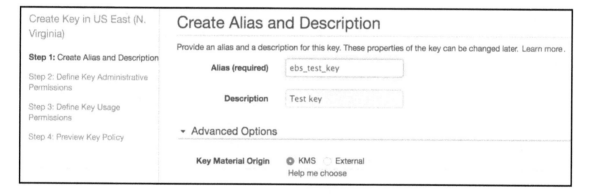

Then you can define who can manage the key:

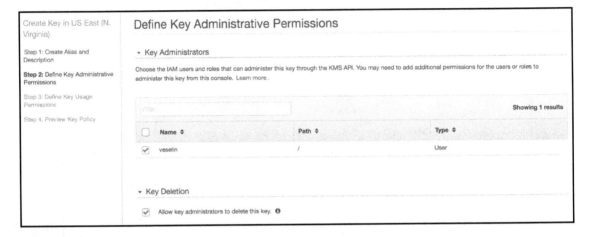

As well as who can use it:

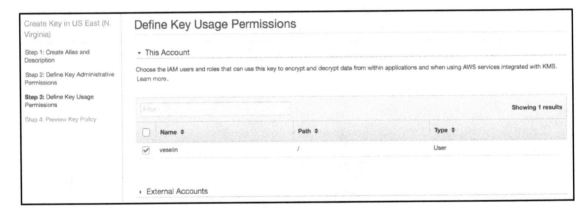

And the result should be visible back on that dashboard among the list of keys:

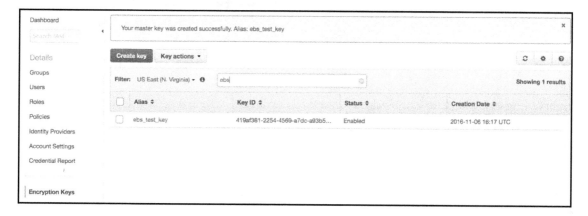

Now if you were to switch to the EC2 Console and choose to create a new EBS volume, the custom encryption key should be available as an option:

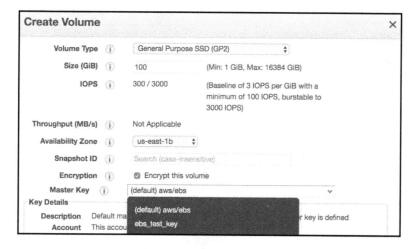

You can now proceed to attach the new encrypted volume to an EC2 instance as per the usual process.

S3 objects

S3 allows the encryption of all, or a selection of objects within a bucket with the same **AES-256** algorithm as EBS here.

A few methods of key management are available (ref:
`http://docs.aws.amazon.com/AmazonS3/latest/dev/serv-side-encryption.html`):

- You can import your own, external set of keys
- You can use the KMS service to generate custom keys within AWS
- You can use the S3 service default (unique) key

Encrypting existing data can be done on the folder level:

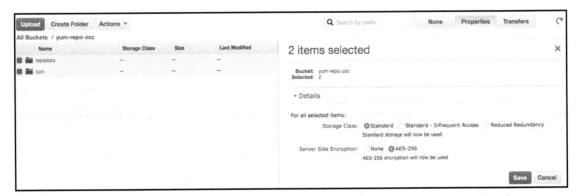

or by selecting individual files:

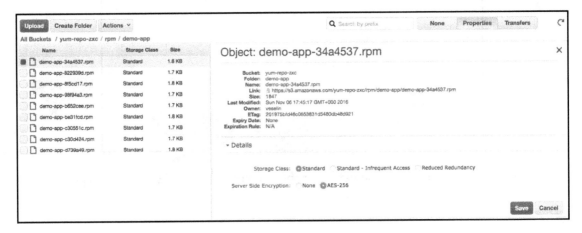

New data is encrypted on demand by either specifying a header (`x-amz-server-side-encryption`) in the PUT request or by passing any of the `--sse` options if using the AWS S3 CLI.

It is also possible to deny any upload attempts which do not specify encryption by using a bucket policy (ref:
`http://docs.aws.amazon.com/AmazonS3/latest/dev/UsingServerSideEncryption.html`).

OS updates

If you follow any security bulletins, you would have noticed the frequency with which new security flaws are being published. So, it is probably not much of an exaggeration to state that OS packages become obsolete days if not hours after a fully up-to-date EC2 instance has been provisioned. And unless the latest vulnerability is affecting BASH or OpenSSL, we tend to take comfort in the fact that most of our hosts reside within an isolated environment (such as a VPC), postponing updates over and over again.

I believe we all agree this is a scary practice, which likely exists due to the anxiety that accompanies the thought of updating live, production systems. There is also a legitimate degree of complication brought about by services such as **Auto Scaling**, but this can be turned to an advantage. Let us see how.

We'll separate a typical EC2 deployment into two groups of instances: *static(non-autoscaled)* and *autoscaled*. Our task is to deploy the latest OS updates to both.

In the case of static instances, where scaling is not an option due to some application specific or other type of limitation, we will have to resort to the well-known approach of first testing the updates in a completely separate environment then updating our static production hosts (usually one at a time).

With Auto Scaling however, OS patching can be a much more pleasant experience. You will recall Packer and Serverspec from previous chapters, where we used these tools to produce and test AMIs. A similar Jenkins pipeline can also be used for performing OS updates:

1. Launch the source AMI.
2. Perform a package update.
3. Run tests.
4. Package a new AMI.
5. Proceed with a phased deployment in production.

To be comfortable with this process, we certainly need to put a decent amount of effort into ensuring that tests, deployment and rollback procedures are as reliable as practically possible, but then the end justifies the means.

Security auditing

AWS offers some good tools to help you keep your security policies in shape. Those will provide you with detailed audit reports including advice on how to improve any potential risk areas. In addition, you can configure service logs, so you get a better understanding what goes on within your deployment or AWS account as a whole.

VPC Flow Logs

This service lets you capture information about the network traffic flowing through a VPC. The generated logs (unfortunately not quite real-time yet) contain src/dst port, src/dst address, protocol and other related details (for a full list please see: `http://docs.aws.amazon.com/AmazonVPC/latest/UserGuide/flow-logs.html#flow-log-r ecords`). Apart from making for some pretty cool graphs to help identify network bottlenecks, the data can also be used for spotting unusual behavior. You could, for example, devise an in-house IDS by parsing the **Flow Logs** and forwarding any suspicious entries to your monitoring solution.

In the VPC Console, select a VPC and switch to the **Flow Logs** tab:

Click on **Create Flow Log**: you will need to fill a few parameters such as the IAM Role to be used (click on **Set Up Permissions** to create one) and the desired name of the **Destination Log Group**.

In a few minutes, the said log group should appear under the **Logs** section in the **CloudWatch** dashboard:

Within that group, you will find a log stream per EC2 instance (per network interface to be more precise) containing the captured traffic details.

CloudTrail

The **CloudTrail** service is used for recording API activity within an AWS account. This includes requests done via the AWS Console, the CLI, the SDK or other services which issue calls on your behalf. The trail can be helpful for both security auditing and troubleshooting. Collected data is stored in S3 as encrypted objects, along with signed hashes to help ensure no tampering has occurred.

To enable the service, we go to the **CloudTrail** dashboard looking for a **Get Started** or an **Add new trail** button:

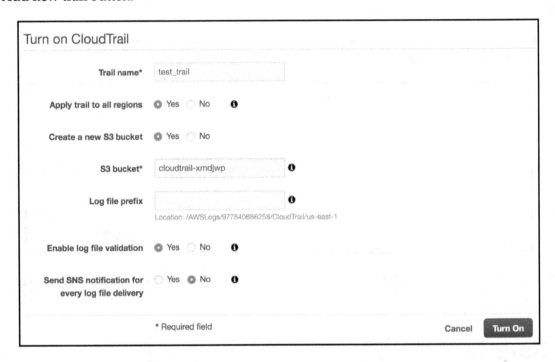

We have chosen to collect data from all regions, storing it in a new S3 bucket with validation turned on. It is also possible to receive notifications on each log delivery, which can be useful for any further processing jobs.

Back on the dashboard, we click on the new trail to review its settings:

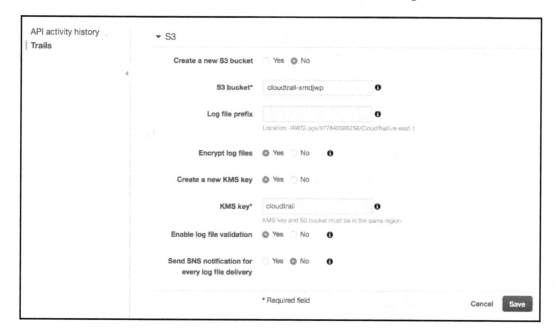

We enable encryption, then enter a name for the new KMS key. After approximately 15 minutes, we should see events appearing under the API activity history dashboard tab:

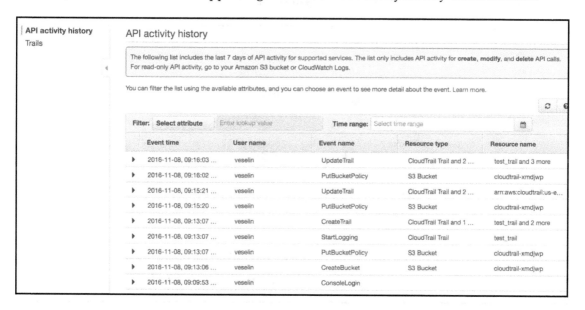

Expanding any of these entries would provide additional information such as the `access_key` used for the given API call and source IP.

In the S3 bucket we would find two subfolders: **CloudTrail** which holds the API logs and **CloudTrail-Digest** for the file hashes.

Trusted Advisor

The **Advisor** is enabled by default and periodically reviews your AWS account in order to identify any risk or areas of improvement.

It provides insights about cost, performance, security and HA as seen on the dashboard:

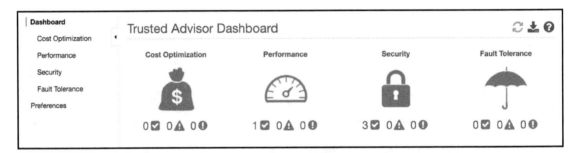

We are mainly interested in the security tips at this time:

Things appear to be green, following the steps we took to secure the root account earlier in the chapter.

In addition to this view, weekly e-mail reports can be configured under the **Preferences** tab.

AWS Config

With **Config** we can track, inspect, and alert on resource changes that have occurred within our deployment.

When first enabled, the service performs an inventory of the resources found within the region and starts recording any changes.

Once a resource change is detected, for example a new rule is added to a security group, Config allows us to view a timeline with details about the current and any previous changes to that resource.

Another powerful feature is change inspection. Within Config we can define a set of rules to be evaluated against each resource change and alerts generated where necessary.

Let us try both use-cases.

Click on **Get Started** on the Config dashboard, then choose a **Bucket name** and a **Role name**:

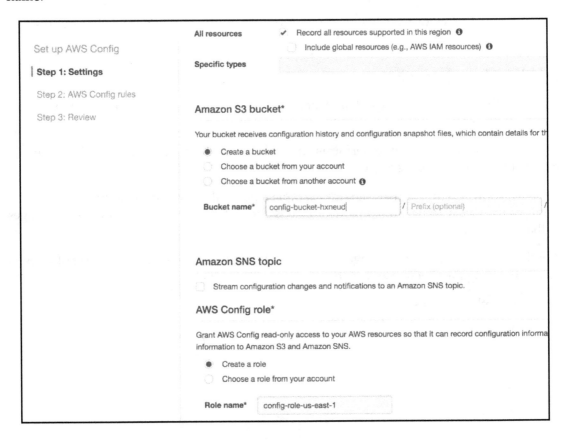

One the next page we can choose a few rules to get us started:

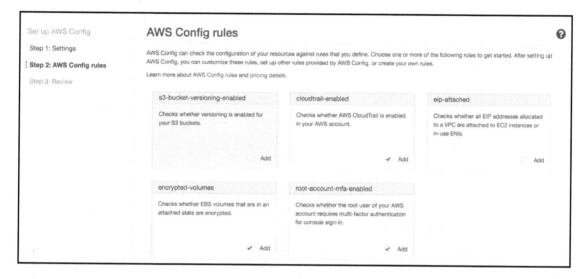

We have chosen to monitor CloudTrail, EBS volumes and MFA settings. Finalize the setup and go back to the **Rules** tab in the dashboard where we can add some more.

 Please note that at the time of writing, there is a cost of $2 per active rule per month.

Click on **Add rule** and look for the **restricted-ssh** rule which will monitor security groups for open SSH access. With the new rule in place, we can make a few resource changes and see how Config reacts to these. As an example, disable CloudTrail and create a temporary security group which allows incoming SSH from anywhere.

After a short while we can see the effect on the **AWS Config** dashboard:

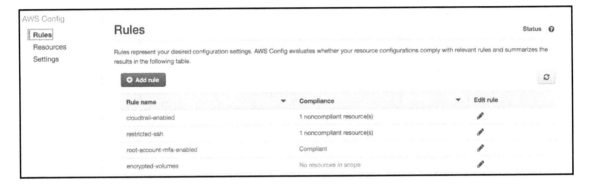

We can click on the **restricted-ssh** entry for more details. Locate the noncompliant entry in the list and click the **AWS Config** timeline icon:

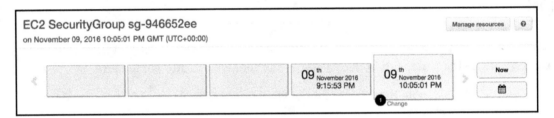

We can see the two recorded states of the resource. Clicking on the **Change** shows us what has happened:

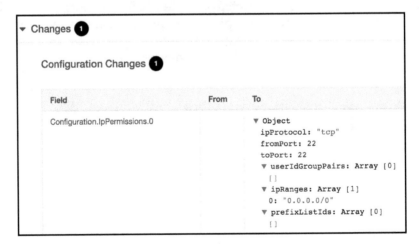

Here we see the reason why our security group resource has been flagged as **noncompliant**.

In addition to the AWS-provided Config rules, you could write your own in the form of Lambda functions (ref: `http://docs.aws.amazon.com/config/latest/developerguide/evaluate-config_develop-rules.html`).

Self pen testing

Here we examine self pen testing as an inexpensive alternative or as a preparation step prior to you hiring a third party for the official test (considering that each penetration testing iteration is usually chargeable).

The goal is a system which allows for on-demand and/or regular vulnerability scanning against our VPC deployment both internally and externally.

Two community projects that can help us with this task are **OpenVAS** (ref: `http://www.openvas.org`) and **OpenSCAP** (ref: `https://www.open-scap.org`).

A relatively easy way of setting up such an automated scanner would be to use a prebaked AMI and some user data. In essence, you would install either or both of the preceding frameworks on a vanilla EC2 instance and create an AMI out of it. Then launch a new instance of that AMI (perhaps per schedule) and, using user data, you would start the scanner, pass it the destination URI to be scanned, then e-mail any scan reports or save to S3.

Scheduling is achieved using an Auto Scale Group, which simply launches a node, then terminates it after N hours (however long it takes to perform the scan). Alternatively, you could use CloudWatch events together with some Lambda functions (ref: `https://aws.amazon.com/premiumsupport/knowledge-center/start-stop-lambda-cloudwatch`).

 Please note that vulnerability scanning or similar activity needs to be approved by AWS Support first (ref: `https://aws.amazon.com/forms/penetration-testing-request`).

Following the advice throughout this chapter is one step towards creating a more secure environment, but we can by no means consider the job done. It has been said that security is a process, not a product and as such it should perhaps be a daily task on one's list.

It is recommended that you subscribe to relevant security feeds or mailing lists.

AWS maintains a few of its own:

- `https://aws.amazon.com/blogs/security`
- `https://aws.amazon.com/security/security-bulletins/`
- `https://alas.aws.amazon.com/`

Summary

In this chapter we covered some ideas on how to improve the overall security of an AWS account.

We looked at AWS services which can be used for auditing and alerting on suspicious activity plus open-source tools that can be useful for regular vulnerability scanning.

In the next chapter we will look at a list of popular (and less so) AWS tips and tricks.

10

AWS Tips and Tricks

In this chapter, I would like to provide you with a selection of random bits of advice. Some of them are derived from my own experience with using AWS; others are found in the AWS whitepapers or related blogs.

A few links on the subject:
https://d0.awsstatic.com/whitepapers/AWS_Cloud_Best_Practices.pdf
https://wblinks.com/notes/aws-tips-i-wish-id-known-before-i-started/
https://launchbylunch.com/posts/2014/Jan/29/aws-tips/

Using VPCs

Apart from the initial, minor setup overhead, it is generally accepted that you are better off deploying your infrastructure inside a VPC. AWS even provides you one by default and tends to deploy resources in it unless you ask otherwise. A VPC gives you more flexibility when operating EC2 instances, better control of your networking, and enhanced security. Also, it is free.

Keep the Main route table as a fallback

If you follow the previous tip, you will notice that a new VPC comes with a route table marked as **Main**:

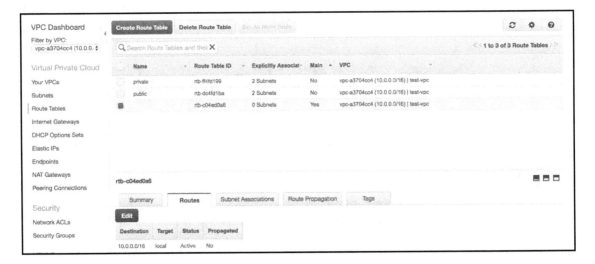

I would recommend that it is left as it is, with a single, local route, and create additional route tables for any custom routing needs instead.

This way, the main or default route table becomes a sort of a safety net for any subnets that get created but remain unassociated, be it by mistake or intent.

Staying within the VPC

As tempting as it may be, try to avoid exposing your VPC resources, as this defeats the purpose. This is to say, instead of assigning public IPs to your EC2 instances, which might give you quick and easy access, use a designated ssh-gateway host (also known as a bastion or a jump host) to hop through.

You would assign a public (Elastic) IP only this single machine, ensure its security group is locked down to the static IPs of your home and/or work place, and use it to connect (say over ssh) to any other instances within your VPC.

Creating IAM roles in advance

We have already discussed EC2 instance roles as a much better way of providing credentials to your application.

A good practice is to always create and assign an IAM role to your instances, even if it is not needed at the time and holds no permissions.

This is because IAM roles can only be assigned when an EC2 instance is being launched.

Groups over users

As you create your first deployment, you might not necessarily have that many users needing access to your AWS account.

Nevertheless, it is still a good idea to assign permissions to an IAM group and make your IAM users members of it, as opposed to granting privileges to each user as they come.

In the long term, it is often the case that team members tend to require (reuse) the same list of permissions.

Knowing the AWS service limits

An AWS account comes with certain limits that can be found in the AWS console:

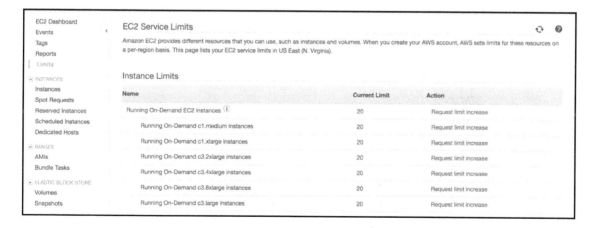

These are meant to protect the customer as well as the provider against any unintentional use. The following are examples:

- A coding error in your CloudFormation template, resulting in an unexpected amount of storage or other resources being provisioned
- A misconfigured Auto Scaling Group, launching tens or hundreds of instances
- Your user making an API call to request an unusual number of instances

As we can see, the said limits are an overall good idea, most of the time.

If you find yourself in a production environment, getting ready for a major event and the traffic spike that comes with it, you certainly want to be aware of your current AWS service limits. Most instance types are initially limited to 20, VPC EIPs to 5, and storage types to 20 TB.

Ideally, you would review these as soon as you get an idea of your expected usage baseline (allowing for bursting) and contact AWS Support requesting a limit increase where needed.

Pre-warm ELBs if needed

On the subject of traffic spikes, while ELBs are impressively performant, there might be occasions where you will need to pre-warm them.

As you probably already know, an ELB is a collection of EC2 instances managed by AWS, running proprietary load balancing software.

An algorithm ensures that the number of ELB EC2 instances grows or shrinks in response to the traffic pattern of your application. This process of adaptive scaling is done based on averaged traffic measurements taken over time and as such is not very rapid.

To ensure that this feature does not become a problem, AWS allows you to request an ELB to be pre-warmed, that is to say, scaled-up ahead of time.

If you are on the premium support plan, you could probably wait until a few hours prior to the event; otherwise, you should contact the support team sooner to account for the extra response time.

You will be asked a series of questions relating to the expected requests per second, average payload size, event duration, and other traffic properties, which will help AWS Support determine whether pre-warming is necessary at all.

Using termination protection

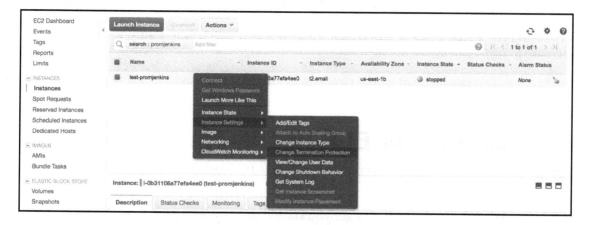

It goes without saying that one should not keep state on machines if it can be helped.

After all, the beauty of AWS is that it allows you to not focus so much on individual instances any more. It promotes a cluster or service culture where the health of the endpoint is of importance.

For the rare cases where we must have one of those management or similar type of non-autoscaling node, however, you have nothing but to gain from protecting yourself against accidentally making the wrong API call or a console click.

Tagging what you can

This sounds like a chore, but it does indeed pay back later. Whether for the much better clarity on your AWS bill or the extra flexibility you get when managing your resources, tags are always useful.

Instrument your tools to apply tags whenever an asset is provisioned, then start scanning your estate regularly for any untagged resources.

Deploying across multiple zones

Unarguably, deploying within the same physical location should yield the lowest latency.

In the majority of use cases however, the added few milliseconds in return for a multiple increase in resilience are worth it.

Try to span your deployment across two availability zones at least.

Enhancing your ELB health-checks

The stock ELB health checks allow you to check raw TCP responses or go higher in the stack and look for an HTTP/200 response.

Either is good. A basic check should get you started but as your application and its dependencies evolve, you might need to enrich your health checks too.

Let us suppose that you were serving a web application that relies on a cache and a database backend.

If the ELB was checking `TCP:80` then as long as your HTTP daemon is running, it will receive an OK. If you were checking for an HTTP/200, instead that would verify access to the application's file(s) on disk but likely not much more.

Instead, you could benefit much more from pointing the ELB at a dedicated health check endpoint within your application, which verifies all its dependencies (disk: OK, cache: OK, db: OK) before returning a green light. But beware of impacting the overall application performance: the more frequently the health check is called, the more lightweight it ought to be.

Offloading SSL onto the ELB

AWS now issues free SSL certificates as part of the **Certificate Manager service** which also takes care of renewals. This seems like a pretty good reason on its own.

Managing certificates on the ELB itself is much more convenient in comparison to doing the same across a number of EC2 backend instances. Also, there must be at least a small amount of CPU performance to be gained by delegating the SSL operations.

EIP versus public IP

A few points about the two types, in case you have not used these much.

Public IPs:

- You choose whether an instance should have a public IP at the time you are launching it
- The address will persist across reboots but not a stop/start
- These come at no extra cost

Elastic IPs:

- You can associate/disassociate an EIP with an instance at any time after it has been launched
- An EIP remains associated across reboots or start/stop operations
- EIPs incur cost (when kept unused)
- EIPs can be migrated between EC2 instances

In light of the IPv4 deficit we are facing today, AWS is cleverly trying to incentivize sensible provisioning by charging for any dormant EIP resources.

Be a gentleman/lady and release your IPs when you are done with them.

Mind the full-hour billing

It is great that AWS allows you to pay-for-what-you-use and as-you-go. Something to keep in mind, however, is that AWS meters usage in hourly increments.

So, say you were running a number of batch jobs, launching and terminating an instance every 10 minutes. After an hour and 10 minutes, you would have launched and terminated six instances (6x smallest increment of 1h) resulting in 6 hours of billable usage despite the fact the neither of them lasted more than 10 minutes.

At any rate, to avoid surprises, it is highly recommended you to set up billing alerts. These are simple CloudWatch alarms which can notify you when your estimated bill has reached a threshold.

Using Route53 ALIAS records

This is a special in-house type of DNS record specific to the Route53 service.

For an AWS user an Alias record is a great alternative to a CNAME (for supported resources).

Some of the main advantages are:

- Aliases resolve directly to an IP address, saving the extra lookup which a CNAME would require
- Alias records are supported at the zone apex, so you could create an alias which uses the top of a domain (for example `mydomain.com`)
- Alias records allow advanced Route53 features such as weighted/latency/geo routing and failovers
- There is no AWS cost associated with Alias lookups

NB: A Route53 Alias record can currently only point to a limited set of AWS resources. For more information please see: `http://docs.aws.amazon.com/Route53/latest/DeveloperGuide/resourc e-record-sets-choosing-alias-non-alias.html`

The S3 bucket namespace is global

This means that if you get a name conflict when creating a bucket, it is likely because somebody else in the AWS universe has beaten you to it.

Devise a naming schema that offers some uniqueness; perhaps, use your organization's name or a random prefix/suffix to the bucket name.

S3 bucket deletion tends to propagate slowly. Pay attention to the region in which you are creating your bucket. If you get it wrong, you will need to delete then wait for 20-30 minutes in my experience before you can recreate it in the right place.

– versus . in the S3 bucket name

It seems that there is often the question of whether one should name buckets as `images-example-com` or `images.example.com`.

Two things to consider are:

- Would you like to use S3 over HTTPS?
- Would you like to use a custom domain name instead of the default S3 bucket URL?

Strictly speaking, buckets with dots in the name will show an SSL mismatch warning when you address them over HTTPS using the default bucket URI.

This is due to the fact that S3 operates on the `.amazonaws.com` domain, and any extra dots will make it seem as if a bucket is a subdomain (not covered by the SSL certificate).

On the other hand, you have to use dots if you want to have a custom domain (CNAME) pointed at your bucket. That is to say, the bucket name has to match the said custom URL in order for S3's virtual-host style service to work.

For example, we call our bucket `images.example.com` and add a DNS record of `images.example.com` CNAME `images.example.com.s3.amazonaws.com`.

S3 would then forward incoming request to any bucket with a name matching the host in the HTTP headers (refer to
`http://docs.aws.amazon.com/AmazonS3/latest/dev/VirtualHosting.html`).

So, it would seem that based on the name we chose, we can use either one of the features or the other (HTTPS vs CNAME). But there is a solution to this dilemma: CloudFront.

Placing a CloudFront distribution in front of our bucket allows a custom domain, plus a custom SSL certificate, to be specified.

Randomizing S3 filenames

An important fact is that S3 takes filenames (object keys) into consideration when distributing data. You are likely to get better performance when your content does not use a sequential naming convention. For more details on the distribution mechanism please refer to
`http://docs.aws.amazon.com/AmazonS3/latest/dev/request-rate-perf-considerations.html`

Initializing (pre-warm) EBS volumes

It used to be the case that all EBS storage was meant to be initialized to avoid the first-time-access penalty, which becomes a noticeable overhead as you start dealing with larger and larger volumes. Nowadays, the situation has improved as new volumes need no pre-warming (ref: `http://docs.aws.amazon.com/AWSEC2/latest/UserGuide/ebs-initialize.html`); however, one should still consider the added delay to the boot process (if the volume is needed at boot time) against any potential performance gains.

For very large volumes, initialization might be prohibitive, but in any other case, it is certainly worth doing. Or if you run your own database servers on EC2, then you should definitely consider pre-warming volumes regardless of size.

You could use the suggested command-line steps to measure time spent performing this type of optimization (refer to `http://docs.aws.amazon.com/AWSEC2/latest/UserGuide/ebs-initialize.html`).

Summary

In this chapter, we looked at some tips, tricks, facts, and general information, which are useful to keep in mind when using AWS.

This is naturally just a small selection of such public secrets, and if you are also excited about the peculiarities of the AWS environment plus the creative hacks that users come up with to work around them – I would recommend you to check out `https://aws.amazon.com/blogs/aws/`.

Index

W